Island Eyes
CLEM

Welcome to Island Eyes. In it you will find my True-Life hedonistic tale of travel, adventure and delusion, interwoven with a spiritual fantasy and a story of a little crab who followed his dream ...

57 chapters of true-life Island Eyes
19 scenes from god-like eyes
6 episodes through eyes on stalks

This is not how I planned it – it's just what happened ...

Island Eyes
CLEM

ISBN 978-1-909936-26-3

The main chapters of this book are a true story – where necessary names have been changed or omitted to protect people, hopefully, still living.

The sections under Lemon and Crab are entirely fictitious and any resemblance to real persons, creatures or deities, living or dead, is purely coincidental.

Published 2019
Pendown Publishing
Cornwall, United Kingdom

Set in 12pt Gentium BB

www.pendownpublishing.co.uk

Dedication

To all those who said I should write about that time in my life and to all who have helped and hindered this story - thousands of thanks!

I said it would be done by Christmas - I just didn't know which Christmas.

I wrote a book for you all - and this is it.

Acknowledgements

For constant motivation, proof-reading and correcting my terrible grammar - when it had to be done to make sense - thanks go to my Mum, Carly, Alexa and Nina.

Other huge thanks go to everyone else who kept me up all night and on the beach all day, postponing the release date as far as we could stretch it - because the good times are always worth it.

Chapter 1 – blue veins

I had cuts, slits. Splits in my fingertips. Chapped lips.

The storm was vile, hitting the high notes of turmoil. I was near laughter, treading the line of desperate hysteria that comes as a last resort.

The moon stretched oval through sheet rain, a dramatic backlight to the shadow-puppet mosh-pit of palm trees writhing in the typhoon. This scene was heavy with consequences, a copy-paste, from an Ancient Greek mythological clusterfuck of the elements.

Blue turned to warm red on the inside of my leg. Blood met with hot rain and Thor struck the ocean. I took a mental image in the lightning whitewash.

Well-worn climber's fingers helped crimp the corrugated steel over the ridge of the roof, mere minutes before it had been ripped loose and now it strained against my grip, I struggled against each suppressed kick. The bones in my fingertips pressed hard against the metal through weak pressure-numb skin; willing the steel to stay in place.

I cast a look to the unnamed mountains leering ominously over a town in torment. 'This carnage, *did you do this*!?' Swift rebuke was doled out by unseen forces; in a second my fingers slipped and the sound of tearing punctuated the sky. The metal prisoner released itself from my grasp and left a trail of blood-red on exposed skin. Burning pain seared from thigh to chest and I fell to my knees in a wonderfully pure moment of shock.

My meagre material possessions lay together below me, my poor showing of life on the island. Any false move would render me homeless by morning. With new nerve I dug my feet deep into wet straw, straightened and inhaled the storm. The rain tasted wrong, mangled, in my heightened animal state. My skin was vibrating with the need to pin this beast, my lips were quivering with an animal roar to challenge the deafening storm.

Blink. Moonlight bled into my vision as a drop clung and skipped from lash to lid

The storm must have sensed I was about to make my move and, before I could act, the metal sheet was hit with a swift uppercut of wind. The space between us became thick with debris as heavy spray flew from its mane, this insurmountable beast, its back cracking and razor-hooves circling in the wind. For one glorious moment it stood tall before it twisted to the right throwing air from its underside.

My adrenaline reached its crescendo as the blade silently dropped, cutting the night in two. Sheet steel hit straw at an angle, spitting salt into my strained eyes and inflaming open wounds. This was my chance, the blunt ridge of the fold momentarily exposed. This second was my slim chance.

My head, ever the forward thinker, pulled back to protect my face from being split in two. My hands, however, lived for the moment and seized it - without permission - they reached out and slapped down hard on the metal backbone, pinning the sheet and taking control once more.

This! This was an unforgettable feeling; seated upon the folded sheet, atop the bamboo hut on the forsaken island, in the middle of an unbelievably biblical storm. The rain tapped a drum-roll, feeding into my numbed veins, leading up to the realisation of my situation.

What do you do when you clamp a crocodile's jaw, but don't have a rubber band? My hands were empty and I felt a chuckle threaten to burst through sore lips; the only thing keeping the roof on my house - was the body seated upon it - dappled in mud, blood and straw, drowning in thin air. Laughing to myself, real laughter this time, I finally felt alive. Real life - pushing through blue veins.

Chapter 2 - before we knew any better

Welcome to the procrastination generation. For the most part the lights were out. These rooms had no walls and a million windows. Behind each chat a face glows blue in the backlight. Teenagers trip on their words as flirting Japanese businessmen crouch behind a cut-and-paste supermodel face, catfish to the taste.

We were the first to watch a boob load from top to bottom. One. Line. Of. Pixels. At. A. Time. Adolescent discovery would freeze mid-nipple by the ominous click of a phone being lifted off its dialling block. We thought money was good, drugs were bad and 'stop, drop and roll' was the right thing to do when on fire.

There we sat, paying attention to things that help no one and mean nothing. We were the youth of the western world and we were obsessed with distracting ourselves from mediocrity so naturally we worked on making our language as confusing as possible. Rather than typing out fully formed words it was unanimously decided that we would randomly jumble letters together. We started to LOL at people through type; it worked well, laughing out loud without parting lips, all the time it seemed, guffawing to ourselves in the darkness.

We abbreviated our shock and blasphemy. Choosing WTF, back when we didn't know how often it would apply. The BRB saved us millions of seconds and OMG came in handy so American teens would finally have something to say, in their own distracting way - you see, by now we had realised that someone could just make stuff up and it might just catch on.

Soon we were wielding the power held by a four letter acronym. From the deepest philosophies of modern day scholars and the seven tones of dial-up we unveiled 'MILF!' As footballers became fathers the girls screamed 'DILF!' Spot a timeless classic by its royal roots, watch a coronation turn a PILF into your highness; the QILF! The power of the quadcronym was unstoppable by now; the world seemed a veritable orgy of almost words, a cacophony carnival. Lights were flashing, babies were crying! What the hell is a LMAO? Did they just insult me or have they finally passed out on the keyboard? The evolution was all-powerful as threes become fours become fives. Before you know it a LOL is a LMAO is a LMFAO. The madness was insatiable and we thought it mattered!
It didn't.

The hieroglyphs of this millennium push the boundaries of logic; they burst the seams of their intended application. We were the uncensored narcissistic opinionated globally enlightened *sticky* fingered mouth-breathing generation of the internet. Ultimately we would spend a lot of time reading quotes online.

Then it got weird.

I remembered it like it was yesterday; face to face with the glare of the mini-fridge size monitor, training my eyes to rely forever on glasses. Hours go by as the internet broke me into the issues of the outside world, worries that weren't, people who were. As a Christian-family child in a farming community I was not exactly rife with worry or self-doubt. Good grades, health and burning in Hell were the height of my concerns. As you can imagine some things the internet had in store could be a little confusing.

Sender: MaxManhood

Subject: GET A REAL MAMMOTH IN YOUR PANTS

Mental images of mammoths in pants went down well and 'Max Manhood' knew how to get a hold of one, this was a surprise to me. I opened the email.

Racing red block capitals shouted; *'Double your size and last for hours in bed.'* Why?

I was already a sound sleeper, lasting a good eight to ten hours without a stir, and about this disproportionate growth serum on offer ... entertaining though it may be there would inevitably be some lifelong logistic difficulties - taking a bath came to mind. Turns out Max hadn't thought this one through.

Scroll down, freeze. Yes they had trunks, but this selection of flesh tripods were far from woolly. Nope.

It turns out Max was a bit of a creep. I looked down, I looked up.

Why the hell? Try as I might a comparison was hard not to make and a small crack began to appear in my childish content. Well done, Max. Still, top work on the sleeping pills.

Chapter 3 – paint by numbers

I lived on a Cornish smallholding, which is like a small farm that doesn't make money. My parents believed in God, I'm not sure why, or if they still do. It's not important I guess. They also believed in education, both being teachers in a nearby school, my three older brothers and I were expected to take our studies very seriously, and we did. I worked hard, learning how to pass exams with that inside-the-box mentality the British curriculum expects of you.

I used to scribble way over the lines, colouring the snowman's nose green, pink windows on a turquoise fire engine, snapping crayons as I slammed purple apples on the rainbow tree, at least that's how I remembered it - and it was as fun then as it is now.

So another day started the same way, the teacher gave the entire class a new colouring task; colour in the thing on the paper and then give it back. It was the same stencil as I'd seen before, pretty much, but with a little number in the corner of each section.

The idea here, she explained, is that these numbers would tell you which paint you put on which part of this picture... 'See there,' she chirped, pretending she didn't hate us all, 'Number two is Orange.' Dot. Dot. Dot; a sea of blank faces. She leaned in, 'See that little number two on the snowman's nose? Number two is orange, so now you colour the snowman's nose orange. Okay?' I remember wanting to ask why, but I went with the easy answer, and said, 'Okay!'

So the snowman's nose became orange and no damage was done.

Using this method of making sure the thing on the paper is what was supposed to be on the paper, I managed to turn myself into a good student. Really good at times - depending who I was copying from.

The problem with this system was that no matter how intent I was in hiding the fact that I didn't understand anything at all, plastic chairs and scratching chalk just weren't all that exhilarating. I found myself day-dreaming a lot. 'CAN YOU TELL ME, BOY?!' A voice bellowed in my face. Oh hell, did I just pee myself?

The headmaster shook as the blood left his feet to become a professional tomato-face, holding a menacing stare but dropping the volume he continued, 'WHAT is outside the window that YOU seem to find so much more fascinating than MY lesson?' The problem with shouting in someone's face is that it doesn't make them listen, it makes them hate you.

'WELL?' His stupid face shook like a bulldog running up the stairs.

Now then. I really wanted to answer this question honestly and say 'everything!' Or go so far as to elaborate with something like, 'everything you aggressive, moronic dick. Everything out there is better than everything in here.' Instead I lied and said I was sorry.

What did I learn? Basic survival skills of course. Mastering the art of taking notes when the teacher was asking questions and to turn over the blank paper only to start mid-sentence just as he or she would glide past by my desk. Armed with these skills, and a lack of an explanation why anyone would be finding 'x' in the first place, I would set about a task with the initial aim of finding a way out or a quick fix.

So came the exams and I cheated as hard as I could.

Year after year. I'm not saying I didn't learn something aside from the art of manipulation, but this system seemed a little flawed. It was as though someone somewhere just had it in for me and was determined to waste my time, forcing me to stare at some paper for three hours a week until I still couldn't speak French. Dommage.

Some days when they were feeling particularly sadistic they made me sit in a silent exam hall for ages while I tried to show them how much I understood, only to discover that staring isn't the same as learning after all.

This is the way I spent entire years of my life, finding ways to pretend I knew what was going on until the bell rang, and I'm not bitter about that. Not at all.

Lemon - scene 1

'What are you doing?'

'Nothing.' My eyes welled. They did this anytime I was confronted without warning.

'I've seen you here before, boy.'

I knew the voice, they called her Lemon, and I never thought she would be interested in talking to someone who was, well, who was like me.

A twig cracked behind me, I wasn't ready for this. Pulling the sheet down as carefully as I could, I tucked the edges around it - just in time?

'Hello?' She was so close to me, too close for me - it felt like someone was blowing into my eyes. I was so nervous, why does this happen?

'Please go away.' I spoke into my hands. Trying to breathe steadily.

'What's your name?' She was entirely too close, I didn't want to breathe too hard in case she could hear.

'What is it you are looking at, I want to see.'

I felt her right next to me, I didn't want this. I found myself staring into the back of my own head.

'It's okay...' She spoke softly. She must have heard my breathing.

It wasn't okay, blood rushed in my eardrums; I can't have this conversation alone. I don't know how.

'I'm not a boy!' I panicked.

'No, you're not at all, I'm sorry.' The way she said it calmed a tiny fragment of the nightmare. I could see her arm in the corner of my eye. I wanted to turn to her but the thought made my throat dry up.

'I know it's hard for you,' she moved her hand a little bit, 'but you can trust me.'

I felt less hot, less like running.

'Will you show me what you've found?' She spoke effortlessly; I was envious of her cool.

'It's not found, I made it.'

Why did I tell her there was anything at all? Did I want her to see, to impress her? Her hand moved slowly over to touch the corner of the sheet, but she didn't lift it. I liked that a lot, that she didn't lift it.

'Will you show me?' Her hand still hovering inches from the edge.

The lump in my stomach eased and I forced myself to mimic her, reaching out and holding the sheet. It was easy enough, it just happened. Together we lifted the cover.

'Oh...' came out in her breath, 'Oh wow!'

My heart pounded. My invention - hovering knee-high above the grass, its tiny atmosphere wrapping around the peaks and troughs. I could feel the chill of the Antarctic on my knees. The light side was alive with many of my millions of species, in my peripheral vision I could see the outline of Lemon – she was just staring at it now. Not moving at all.

'Do you like it?' I whispered, before adding, 'Don't tell anyone.'

Her voice cracked, like mine does sometimes.

'Do I like it?' she repeated, before saying in wonderment, 'This is incredible!'

Chapter 4 – the Great British Mind-set

Years go by and we're still here, most of us anyway. Has it been fascinating? Maybe. For me Portsmouth wasn't quite blowing my mind. I had made it 170 miles up the southern English coastline to a place that was kind-of like home, but 170 miles away. I don't know why I stopped there, I guess it was a little more multicultural and there were fewer farms.

When people generalise and say 'fisherman are like this' or 'Americans think' there is an implied 'some' or 'a lot of' that the listener should attach to the statement as they hear it. If there isn't an 'all' before a statement then we can safely assume it's not an attack on an entire section of society. That being said, British people are a mega downer. Not all, but almost all. I don't think it's their fault, it's just conditioning.

So here I stand, in a supermarket, staring at an old lady. She's too old. I know that, and it would be really easy, but that's not the point. I scanned the aisle for a healthier target with a lower risk of a cod liver oil and prune juice.

Hello, who's this? She's cute, in shape, let's hope that it's from a good diet and not just exercise. I take a stroll in her direction, passing through canned foods, leaving cous cous to my left and pasta on my right. I would just need to take a little sideways glance into her basket to see what I'm dealing with here, and I did. A lot of red items, bell peppers, tomatoes, red onions, this is promising. Wait, abort and keep walking! The edge of a purse was barely visible between spinach and the edge of the basket, but there it was. Now the risk outweighed the reward, I am a thief of time but I didn't want her money.

I walked, thinking about things and stuff, sizing up potential victims. The couple at the end of the aisle? Sure, why not? It would add a bit of diversity into the mix. She was a little fat but that's okay, I can pace myself on her portion. Sandals in the supermarket? I like that. A Greenpeace T-shirt and loose pants pointed to a quinoa and lentil kinda guy. None of these things were a problem, I'm not exactly picky. So I hung back and pretended to admire some seasoning mix, looks pretty good, what are the chances they picked some up too? I wondered if the couple also like spicy food until ... look out, the herd is on the move and coming my way.

I tactically turned to stroll in the same direction, pacing myself so they would naturally overtake me before the junction at the end of the pasta based section. They passed by disconcertingly faster than expected with an air of someone who may have just found their final item and was heading to the checkout – the heist just went from unlikely to impossible.

A wise book once said, '*Stick with it Clem*' so I did just that, keeping a few paces closer this time I followed the couple past frozen foods and into some sort of canned shrine dedicated to college students and alcoholics. As they negotiated their way out of 'microwave meals' I knew that I was in fact right and that wise book was misguided nonsense. I watched them make a beeline towards the shortest checkout line and out of my reach, alas my prize was lost.

But what's this? The basket with a lot of red things, and just feet away, talking on the phone was the girl, purse in hand. This was perfect, good things come to those who wait! I made my move of course - a seemingly meaningless pass between her and her shopping. A stoop and a click gave meaning as the cold metal handles touched in the palm of my hand. I didn't look back as I took the fastest route out of sight, a hard right around some tins of Celebrations and straight for the queue, right in line behind the couple who so recently escaped my ritual.

'Did you bring any of your own bags, sir?'

'Sorry?' The cashier was holding up some micro-thin plastic that was stuck together somehow, 'Oh - no.'

She rung me up. Orange juice £2.25, peppered sheep's cheese £3.00 - that could be interesting - cherry tomatoes £1.49.

I mentally grouped the foods into meals as they passed before me, single iceberg lettuce only one pound, come on bread, make me a sandwich! Tooth brush £3.11, yeah okay. This went on for a while, I paid by card.

So I would live my week on someone else's diet, not every week, but enough to diversify. Sounds unnecessary? That would be because it was unnecessary, but in my defence I discovered some new tastes, found out that there are people who buy three different types of tomatoes from the same shop and that my flatmate could never have too many free tampons.

What about the inconvenience to the people whose groceries I hijacked? This was something I was willing to ignore. Shopping became an act of ninja stealth and as meal time became adventure time the monotonous became *just* a little less so. At one point I tried to recruit disciples, presenting it in such a way as being a social experiment, expanding your palate or just splashing some orange paint on your boring-ass day - but nobody would bite.

The concept of taking something before it's bought and buying it yourself is completely legal, funny and delicious – and still nobody will do it; because it's just not what's done.

The semi-scientific experiment known as Five Monkeys is my favourite portrayal of the great British mind-set, a constant reminder that not everyone belongs in the U.K. and the only explanation I can find why people don't just do whatever they want.

Anyway, it's said that some scientists put five happy little monkeys into a cage that had nothing but a ladder leading up to a bunch of bananas. When one of the monkeys put his hairy foot on the ladder, on his way to eat some tasty bananas, the scientists blasted the monkeys with cold water. This happened every time regardless of which monkey tried, until finally the monkeys stopped going up the ladder and just ate normal boring monkey prison chow instead.

Now it was at this point that the scientists released one of the monkeys from the cage, replacing him with a new monkey, who naturally did what monkeys do and went straight for the bananas. This time the scientists didn't have to use the cold water, because the first four monkeys grabbed the newcomer and beat him up. Yup. After this happened a few times, the new monkey stopped going up the ladder so he wouldn't get beaten anymore.

Then comes the day when the scientists remove another monkey, one of the first four, and replace it with a second new monkey – this time, when the newest monkey moved towards the ladder the other monkeys beat him, even the fourth one joins in even though he has never been blasted with cold water.

So the scientists keep swapping monkeys for new ones, and the gang keeps beating up the new monkey when it goes to eat some bananas, until finally all five monkeys in the cage are new monkeys, and none of them have ever been sprayed with cold water – but still, when a new monkey is introduced they beat him for touching the ladder. The kicker is that they don't actually know why, because the cage has been dry for months.

Why did I tell you that long story about an experiment that may not have even happened? Because everywhere you go and everyone you meet has a little of the final monkey in them. You can ask the Priest why he's a homophobe, or ask the golfer why he wears long socks – it's the same as asking a Brit why they don't want to hijack people's shopping with you or asking the last monkey why he beats up the fresh meat.

The answer is always something like, 'I don't know, it's just how it is' or 'We've always done it this way.' Not for the monkeys and not for you. This shouldn't be an acceptable answer. Still, the mind-set played against my own and like any irritant eventually you have to scratch it or cut that arm clean off.

Chapter 5 - some years later

The familiar buzz precedes a sinking heart; I really hate alarm clocks - those numbers flashing incessantly beside my head. I have my suspicions that these numbers have been following me, ruining good times since that one time they told me to colour that nose orange. Back then I just said okay, and this morning I wondered if I would again. I did.

As it was a weekday the numbers read seven dot four five. Everyone knew this meant *wake up even when you are still very tired*. This was something I never agreed with but, you know, whether you agree of not you say, okay, and get out of bed. Some numbers changed while I was in the shower, beating myself awake, and by the time the clock said nine dot zero zero I was sitting in a chair somewhere.

The years had given me a foam cover on my grey plastic seat but it was still all too familiar. Facing the front, sliding in and out of focus, keeping busy pretending to be busy. Eleven with two zeros meant we could do nothing in a different room for fifteen minutes - but nobody bothered. You could make small talk with the few people more disillusioned than yourself, or you could browse the web, which had come a long way since the mammoth incident.

Refreshing the same page over and over was a good way to pass time, clicking between different windows, closing your browser only to open it again, wishing that just one day a fire would break out so you had a reason to 'Stop, drop and roll'.

Most of the time you don't know you need something until you see an advert for it. I didn't want a self-winding wristwatch just 20 minutes ago – come to think about it I don't think I've ever seen a watch outlive its battery. I don't even know what a thread count is so the next pop-up was a wash, but psychological training for my dog could be good - if I had a dog.

New email received, raise the roof. Click. It seemed the Prince of Nigeria had got himself in a bit of a pickle. Being somewhat familiar with the internet I knew that if you had something really important to say you use AS MANY capital letters as possible. It seems that Prince Al-Hamansi had hit trying times as there was not a lower case letter to be seen. I could sense his desperation. Only a man in dire straits would skip the spell-check and just click send. But, alas for him, I'm not actually that naive. Delete. I don't blame scam artists for trying, but why would I need the prince's fortune when I'm always winning the Bulgarian postcode lottery? I'm surprised he hadn't heard this, all the singles in my area must know already - why else would they all want to meet me? What even is a Zoosk?

One one, dot, zero eight. Time ticks on, the moon face at the next desk opens something putrid and starts funnelling it into the hole above his chin. It smells like food - but not really.

What now? Fly to Thailand from £375!

In three days the £400 in my bank account would be back to somewhere between zero and nothing; the joys of London rent.

I stared at the area between my screen and the wall behind it, both were grey. My mind wandered a little into thoughts of fires breaking out, Bulgarian lottery windfalls and singles in my area.

Then I spent my next month's rent on a one-way ticket to Bangkok. Click.

December 1ˢᵗ
As I fly out I'm pretty excited - slightly nervous and super tired.

The couple in front of me are talking in a code-language known only to the British people; it's a mash-up of complaints and racism. I know it's a secret spy code because nobody would be so world-negative on a flight that goes halfway around it.

Update: the lady just said, 'Knowing our luck it'll be pouring it down when we get there.' They don't seem so unlucky, maybe she has some sort of sickness I can't see. The floral perfume and inch-thick foundation is quite unlucky. I can see her cheek crack a little when she talks.

Conclusion: They aren't unlucky; they are ungrateful.

There is a man in a suit on the plane, it looks really shiny. It's not as shiny as his head. Definitely not as shiny as the Mercedes Benz watch he keeps checking. He makes a funny juxtaposition next to the rude-boy twenty-something trying to lounge in a totally upright chair. He's a bit white for cornrows but at least the backwards cap hides most of that honeycomb zigzag scalp thing he's got going on.

I can't see any other people, but I can hear a family getting settled and some exasperated sighs every time the baby makes one of those cat noises. Kids are cool - I'm not sure why people get so upset about crying babies. Maybe they were never actually a baby themselves and were just born as a fully developed thirty-something asshole.

*'Twist that snap back cap back, mint white, box-fresh Nikes,
stretch out lean back.*
*Wake up it's dark, get home past light. Buy a Merc, pay to
park, early start - early night.*
*Fuck man, just have some kids. Have six - buy a pile of
bricks. Add a breakfast bar to prove a point, I don't know
what - but you do, right?'*
I wrote this. Averagely proud of myself.

Guess what England looks like from a plane ... it
looks like a cloud, you can't even see the country. I
made a good decision.

'They really look like us,' she said, again. 'Tiny lives.'
'Each one has a story,' I told her, 'I mean, they don't live long.'
'How long?'
'Less than a month, but time moves fast in such a small space. It's like their month lasts less than half an hour.'
'That's so sad.' She leaned in close, Lemon had short hair at the back, even shorter than mine is on the sides. 'Can they see us?'
'They can't. No. Well they shouldn't be able to ...' I waved my hand over Europe. 'They don't have the scope.'
'The scope?'
I knew what I meant, scope like telescope, that they didn't have great vision. I just didn't know how to explain it so I blurted instead, 'They aren't very good.'
'They are *very* good,' she reassured me. 'How did you make them seem so ... *independent*?'
'They are independent,' I could feel myself struggling again, 'they breed and breathe and sometimes they even talk about how they got there.'
'But, you said they couldn't see us - but - can they see you?'
'They can't, but some of them know we are here, somehow.' I knew this from when I was reading their books. 'They talk about when they were made.'
'When were they made?'
'Oh, well the people have been there for years.'

'How many years?' She sat back and rested on her heels. 'I thought you said they wouldn't live long enough to remember so far back.'

'Oh no, they don't remember. I'm sure of this.'

She had the most amazing face when she was full of marvel, with diamonds in her eyes and from a white half-smile she let the words come out slowly and carefully, 'They just have a feeling?'

'They get it wrong a lot,' I was scanning the surface and found what I was looking for, 'so this here,' I pointed to one of the more populated land masses, 'these people think that they will have another life after they die, as in they think they come back as someone else, or even one of the animals.'

'That is all kinds of adorable!' Lemon clapped her hands together in pure delight. 'And what else?'

'Umm,' I gently turned the globe towards us. I knew I had to be careful since the one time when I managed to slosh the water everywhere. 'These people here are always telling everyone that after they die they go to another world in the sky.'

She smiled again, looking around the garden theatrically with open palms on her cheeks. 'What, like in the pond or something?'

It wasn't a very good joke but she laughed anyway, so I laughed too.

Chapter 6 – Krung Thep

Bangkok City, late night. A smell like wet gas, if that's possible. The smashed mirror of side-streets were tight and tall, voices sung from cut stone doorways, indecipherable at first.

The broken system of the city that never slept showed me one of its sad sallow faces. She couldn't have been more than sixteen, clutching a child to her chest as she spoke with no rising intonation '... massage.' It was more of a reaction to seeing a tourist than a real question. I tried to look everywhere but in her direction, not knowing what to do. 'Money for baby,' she asked in the same dead tone. I turned and told her I was sorry as I tapped my empty pockets, it was true I didn't have any Thai Baht and if I did maybe this wasn't the street to point out where I kept it.

Shining faces in the lack of light sat back on most doorsteps and although they hung back in the most part, all eyes were on me, the foreigner with the backpack. I left the girl and kept to the centre of the street, but before I was out of earshot she spoke once more, another empty offer, 'Sex?' I didn't look back. This was not my idea of a good time. I pushed on and the street widened until I found myself no longer the only traveller in sight.

Taking turns to attend to weary travellers the girls near the main street had a different approach, 'You want sexy time, mai?' Wide grin. Eyes like quartz. 'Up the bum, no babies.' The temptations of Bangkok backstreets seemed to me to be as close to real sex as a black eye is to mascara. A pasty white man was hesitating, weighing his options. I remember thinking

28

that whatever his choice was, he might find those pockets emptied either way. The rumours I had heard in my pre-flight uninformed chat with two British lads could also be true, let your lust take over common sense on this side of town and you may find a surprise taped back between those thighs. How would you even know until there were two cocks in the room?

'Hey fucker you want massage or not?' The quartz had turned to daggers and that grin was a thin line. I should really stop staring at strangers crotches. 'You not want cunt why you hang about? Cunt!' Okay that was it, my cue to pick up the pace and get the hell out of here. Shaking off the sunken feeling left over from the first encounter and feeling rattled from the last, I told myself that whatever happens to the pasty white man was none of my business and went in search of some brighter streetlights.

I found them, and although I had to stand two feet away from it due to a massive puddle of vomit, I also found a working ATM machine. Toes inches from the run-off I put in a reasonable request for 3000 Thai Baht, which was around sixty pounds and would be enough to last the weekend at least. I pressed the sticky green button for a few seconds until 'Transaction Denied' flickered across the screen.

Did I expect that? Of course I did, the debit card poked back like a mocking tongue. A queue of customers were forming with my nerves. There was nothing that made me more uncomfortable than a reality check. Stabbing 2500 Baht into the keypad was a wishful thought, and was quickly denied. I stood aside for the people behind me, thinking that maybe it was just the machine that was faulty. I knew it wasn't and this was confirmed by a stack of notes spitting out for the next in line. I quietly asked reality to get back in its cage and requested 2000 Baht; it was no more than forty pounds so I thought there was a good chance of success. The two second wait came with an anxious uncertainty, a feeling which I ignored until 'Transaction Denied' flashed across the screen again. I wasn't surprised. I hadn't checked my balance before I left England with the rationalisation that nobody needs another voice with reasons to turn back and give up.

Still I felt good, almost better, there was something beautiful about this point of no return with a touch of 'no other options' and a sprinkle of 'mandatory adventure'. With that thought and a request for 1500 Baht I was met with a 'Please remove your card and await your funds.' An underwhelming thunking sound spat out two notes.

My worldly wealth was a wide silver thousand-baht note and the regal red five-hundred. 'I'll make it last,' I told myself, shoving them deep into my pocket, 'It's simple yeah, just don't spend it.'

The backpacking centre of Bangkok City is known as Khao San Road, a flow of neon funnelling you through a vivid world of what-the-fuck. A kilometre stretch of everything, lined by bars, hotels and hostels with the night-market stalls parked at the forefront pushing and peddling. We are talking real junk here, red Rolex with plastic hands, dollar DVD's and original copy designer clothes. 'Buy bulk condoms, my friend?' 'Real Aviator look good brother?' Incessant offers followed me closely.

I stopped by several sizzling open-stove pans that seemed to stain the air a greasy yellow, pausing to take a closer look. 'Scorpion my friend? Never try, never know.' The black scorpions looked far from edible, tails coiled back and armour shining with cooking oil. I looked up at the speaker who winked and reached behind the upturned milking stool that had a gas canister sat on the underside of the seat, the wok propped precariously atop the three legs. 'I know you brother, you want something special mai? What you want, tarantula very good my price for you Mr...?'

'Just Clem,' I answered, 'but I really can't eat tarantula now, I need ...'

'Scorpion my friend!' I looked up. The vendor had blanked me completely, the new question aimed to a man to my side.

'What you looking?' A new voice came from my other side, it was an elderly woman from the next stall and her face was one big wrinkle. She stood about chest height to me and was definitely the right person to speak to if you wanted to eat crickets and maggots.

'I'm looking for a bed, a cheap place to sleep.'

She nodded, dumping a few handfuls of insects into a paper bowl and handing it to a much younger version of herself. Some loose morsels bounced off the table top and into the gutter, causing a few live versions of the meal to scatter into the open drainage pipe. 'Eat now? I know good room.'

'I don't need good, just cheap.'

The wrinkles shifted into what must have been a smile. 'I know cheap room, eat now?' I pulled my hands back, refusing the offer for now, first things first. The vendor shrugged and gestured to the young helper at her side. 'She my daughter, she find you room, okay?'

The girl turned and smiled, asking, 'Where you go in Thailand?' I didn't have an answer for this, and was only allowed a seconds hesitation before she asked, 'You lost or not? I think lost.'

I thought my answer out carefully, 'I'm not lost, I just don't know where I am or what I'm doing.'

She bounced on the balls of her feet, her face lit up and she laughed, clapping her hands, saying delightedly, 'You lost in Thailand, man, this only Bangkok!' I had only about enough time to laugh and open my mouth before she cut in, 'Not worry guy, everybody lost guy, where did you want to go?'

'I'm looking for a place ...' I said vaguely, unsure of what to specify.

'So you look for place!' She held up a finger then brought it to touch the side of her nose. 'I know the place where you want to go, somewhere just for you guy ...' She paused, I didn't even bother trying to speak this time. What followed was something so in tune with how I felt right then, I couldn't help but lose myself in a huge grin when she followed up with, 'Stay lost and enjoy your life Mister.'

We chatted some more and I asked her where it was I was going and what to expect. She ignored my exact questions, giving me answers like, 'Somewhere that is very good for you,' and, 'In the south, all the way south. Here you can make work no problem, life forever in paradise lost guy ...'

She told me she would find me a ticket to go all the way there, but it would set me back 800 baht. She cocked her head, sizing up my situation. It was actually very cheap but I hesitated out of habit and again she gave me mere seconds before unleashing a barrage of questions. 'Why not? You scared? Only twenty dollar.'

Impulse took me this far and it would have to take me a little farther. In pursuit of sunny shores and barbeque smoke I agreed to take the final step to her mysterious island so I parted my notes in my pocket and handed two thirds of my net worth to the girl. She took it, held it up to the street light and then ran away.

Waiting for her return, I couldn't help hoping I hadn't just bought myself a twenty dollar life lesson in giving money to kids I meet in markets.

The vendor distracted me by waving a dead thing around in my face. 'Try him. Frog!' Once it had stopped waggling I could focus on this single dried-and-fried frog. It didn't look terrible. 'Not money, just for try,' she told me as she delivered the four-legged meal directly to my mouth. I held it between my teeth for a second before biting down, small bones cracking and hard lumps leaking out.

'Very good, no?' It really was. My mouth flooded with a crunchy frog seasoned with salt and cold fat.

She nodded up the road and her granddaughter was there, weaving towards us with my ticket to the mystery island, a blue strip of paper between her fingers.

On the ticket there were three printed boxes, Bus [ ] Boat [ ] Plane [ ] and a selection of times. The first two boxes had a pencil line through them and the time 23:30 was circled. This could be sold as a plane ticket also? Well what the hell, welcome to Thailand I guess!

December 2ⁿᵈ

People have been awake since the first passenger's alarm reminder. The driver introduced himself as 'Dong', pretty funny.

I just went to the bathroom. Mid-pee I noticed I could see the road flying past below me through more than one rusted-out hole in the cubicle floor. I held onto the sink after that, just in case. Now all I can think of is how long it will be until someone finds themselves under the wheels with their pants down.

People keep getting off the bus. I literally have no idea how anyone knows where they are, the bus just stops sometimes and people get off. I still have a solid ten hours ahead of me. I'm not completely sure what I'm doing on this bus but I remind myself that it's really warm on the other side of the window and soon I'll be really warm out there too.

I think the trick here is to ignore anything that gives you doubts.

I can smell my armpits from here.

Chapter 7 – the island

The first step off the boat felt euphoric. My senses sang with the journey's end and reaching the unknown. I felt a disconnection from the world behind my back as the departing boat drew a blade between me and the grey pavements, the junk mail, the 'mind the gap' and the schedule.

I didn't know what I was even doing; staring into this new life. My eyes met with sheer limestone cliffs as they cut eighty feet vertically into vivid gemstone water. The traditional wooden Thai long tail boats were knocking together lazily with the turning tide. A pulsing web of reflections from the sea danced on the underside of wide leaves that hung over the shoreline. I wouldn't have turned away if the world was ending right behind my back.

I really took my time. White sand slid back into my footprints as I trod between the coconut palms. I took breath after breath; faint wood smoke drifting in the tropical haze gave a highly charged buzz and was clearing the jet-lag. These smells and sights were somehow igniting some primal link in the back of my mind.

My heart skipped a beat in preparation for coming to terms with these surroundings. I felt my backpack slide and drop into the sand, letting the low sun's heat deep into my sweat-wet back.

I don't know how long I stood there, paradise wrapping around me, but at some point I must have joined my bag in the sand as I remember the relief in my legs. Sitting, I watched figures crossing my vision as they moved to the shores to watch the sun sink, their outlines slowly turning to silhouettes as the red sky bled across the motionless ocean. An undeniable fog of pheromones hung in the air around them all.

Have you ever had one of those life bumps? It feels like a new realisation in a peaceful moment of thought. When you look at where you are from an outside perspective and you see more than yourself – you see how truly amazing the moment you're living really is. It's as if a tiny balloon of adrenaline in your chest pops and for no more than a few seconds you feel deliriously ecstatic. You're close to laughing but you don't need to, you come back into the world breathless, you feel everything.

I didn't know this feeling before that moment on the beach. Right then everything in the world was perfect.

Lemon - scene 3

'I have to be honest with you.' Lemon was twisting her fingers around one another. What was she doing? It was something I'd done sometimes when I felt, well you know, felt like me.

'Honest? About what?' Sweat prickled through my skin, on my sides and mostly on my forearms.

'I just didn't think you ... Well I actually thought you maybe weren't ... I mean, I had no idea you were so ...' Even I could tell she really wasn't enjoying getting this out, other people's emotions aren't easy for me to read but her struggle was obvious.

'I didn't think you were very clever.' She rushed the space between that, and then this. 'I didn't mean stupid, I meant, well - you never talk.'

I assumed she was feeling right now what it felt like to be me most of the time, never sure if the wrong thing had just come out and how it would be received. 'It's just my condition,' I wanted to make her comfortable again, I didn't know why. 'They told me I will always have trouble making friends.'

'I'm your friend.'

The heat spread over my back and I could feel it filling my face. I had also been told it was rude to turn away when someone was talking to you. I told her the truth of it all in a rush. 'You're different. It's okay with you.'

She was looking right at me and I felt my eyes twinge like they did before they started to water. I pointed at my globe to try to deflect from my rapidly untrustworthy face, 'Hey look at this!' But look at what? I didn't know what I was going to show her, I just needed her to look somewhere else and give me a second to cool off.

'What is that?' She popped back onto her knees and I looked at my finger hovering over the ocean like an idiot. She leaned closer, squinting her face slightly until the edges of her eyes crinkled. 'It's tiny, you mean the island?'

Breathe. Relief. 'Yes, it's one of my favorite places,' I lied. In truth I had never noticed this island before.

'Why is it your favorite place?'

I looked closely, what could I see there? There were people here but not so many of them, and something was missing. 'Cars,' I pointed out. 'There are no cars.'

'It's beautiful, why did you put it all the way out there?'

'Oh no,' I told her, 'the island was pushed up when the sea-bed was still setting, not a design of mine. The people must have got themselves there.'

'I can see why,' Lemon had leant so close her breathing was pushing waves back on themselves. 'Hey look!' She spoke softly in spite of herself, 'They are doing yoga on the beach, in the sand, how funny!'

'Please be careful of the planes, they are easy to ...'

She pulled back instantly, glancing back and placing her hand to her chest. 'I am so sorry, I wasn't thinking. That would have been awful.' She looked genuinely concerned. I decided I wouldn't tell her about the floods. She followed a tiny aircraft over Thailand with her palm flat to the earth, the thumb and smallest finger spread like a plane itself. 'Vrrrrrooooooooom,' she was laughing again. I liked it a lot when she laughed.

Chapter 8 - runner

I woke before my alarm clock. Exhausted before I had even opened my eyes, sick of the dreariness that came with life. I couldn't reach my phone to check the time. My hand stretched up the wall for the light switch but found nothing. My body ached in protest at the thought of leaving my bed for the cold tile floor. I opened my eyes.

They met a close, warm, dusty black. A slice of hard bright light cut under the door and ran a sabre of sunshine along the adjoining wall – the day before suddenly clicked into place. That gap under the door must have been the same one that had let mosquitos in all night.

I wasn't there. I was here. The knot I hadn't realized was clenching in my chest collapsed into relief. I was on an island far away. I looked around for numbers, but there were no alarm clocks in sight! The newfound energy took me right out of the bed, peeling off the thin bedding and rapidly scooping at the clothes on the floor, desperate to feel that glorious sunlight on my skin as soon as possible.

Some people run marathons and others run laps; some people just run in circles their whole life. The difference between a runner and a marathoner is organisation. Marathon running means signing up for a marathon, right? From then on, you prepare for the race. Then at an exact second, sometime months in the future, someone, who isn't running at all, shouts 'Go!' or shoots a gun or something. Then you run for 26.2 miles, or not.

The runner is not the same; I am one of these.
Can we imagine here a fast but deep repetitive beat?
The beat that plays in the runner's mind from time to
time - dropping its first note when that runner wakes
up.

That runner wakes up, sweaty as fuck after a night
of ravaging mosquitoes and such. Squints into the
light that spills under the door of the sweat-box he
booked the night before. With a single bed, the width
of the room, originally white he could assume. The
runner doesn't check the clock; he cracks his neck,
shields his eyes and slides the lock. By the look of the
light it was somewhere vaguely between morning and
night. Not too early. Not too late. He steps out, this
newfound smile on his face and wedges the door back
into place.

So I ran. Like runners do. Up the path I hadn't
been, into the unknown and the unseen.

This is when I met the jungle for the first time ever
and the music delves into a tapping snare.

Here it would seem there was nothing but green.
Sheets of green, tangled around vines, green moss and
slime. Noises came from dark green hollows and
critters shook branches as they chased or followed.
Light that passes through thin wide leaves; sick green
turning a sun beam into a vivid sheen. Okay - so the
path was brown, turning from sand to dirt to broken
rock, half gulley half track.

This was what I had been looking for, no red
rimmed signs saying 'slow' or red lights to say 'no,
don't go.' Not the lines to show you which way to flow,
keep to the limit, speed up, no through.

In time and altitude, running turned to a stumble and my knees started to feel like they were pressing down on a loose tooth. The music dipped to all but nothing letting me take a minute to appreciate the view.

From this peak I had reached I could look down and see the town, pinched like a bow-tie with bays on either side. On one end was the jungle where I sat, fresh and alive, lush shrubbery between the well-trodden paths. The other end was something to behold. The far jungle coated what you couldn't quite call a mountain but more like an extravagant plateau, dense with a much darker and deeper green than what was around me. Small clearings sat on pieces of cliff that had escaped the thick tangle of undergrowth and were jutting out, long valleys sat at the base of it all and spread down towards the town, seen only by the dips they left in the density, still tightly packed with nature's overflow. I could only imagine *what* was creeping and slithering in such a mass that, in places, looked black in the daylight – or, my brain added an afterthought, whom.

December 3rd

I met a girl on my way back from my run. She is a Thai local and called Dow. She walked back down from the jungle viewpoint with me, she might be 25 but I can't tell. I thought she was walking with her son but it turned out it was her younger brother.

She didn't seem surprised when I said I didn't think I would be leaving, apparently a lot of farang come to work here and never leave (Farang is the Thai word for foreigner).

She said, 'You like it here, mai?' Before I answered I asked what a mai was. Dow explained that mai is one of those words that means 'no' or stands as a question mark, depending how you say it. So if you say, 'You want to eat, mai,' it is kind of like, 'You want to eat, no?' but if you said 'mai want to eat', obviously all in Thai, you would be saying that you didn't want to eat. I told her that in that case, yes I liked it here a lot. She said, 'You didn't answer my question, you want to eat, mai?' She seemed pretty easy going so I joined her at her family's home down on the edge of the village.

Her parents' house is amazing; it is just a bamboo hut. Her father showed me all around, even pointing out the toilet and making note that every room had a table. I said 'wow' and 'cool' because I didn't really know what else to say when being presented to a toilet.

Her mother tried to make me really fat in the space of an hour and it was exhausting. From the moment we sat down to eat she filled every gap in conversation by holding different dishes and delicacies in front of my nose. She wouldn't put them down until I had taken a good few ladles from the bowl and she was so happy every time I finished something.

My stomach hurts now and they have asked me to join them tomorrow for a fish barbeque on the beach.

December 4th

The fish BBQ might have turned into an interview. I guess that Dow must have passed on my flimsy living situation to her parents because ten minutes after sitting they were asking me if I would teach their youngest son English. Noi looked like a pudding, all cheeks and tiny black raisin eyes. He had been staring at me all of the last night too, I felt a bit rude for not acknowledging him more so I asked him what he thought about this idea. He didn't say anything, because he doesn't understand English yet. I am an idiot.

After a translation from Dow, Noi looked back at me and shrugged. What did I expect? If some random guy came along and suddenly I had to spend more of my day learning new stuff I wouldn't have been so impressed either.

They told me that if I could teach Noi some basic English and help out sometimes then they could offer me a small bamboo hut to stay in. It was built by their oldest son before he left for the army. It would need some repairs but it would be mine.

Chapter 9 – most of a hut

There are eight little huts by the river, all raised about knee high on short fat bamboo posts, this was to keep the snakes out. Undergrowth from the foot of the jungle crept up to and under most of them, mine had stood abandoned long enough to allow creepers to wrap their way around the posts and occupy most of the rear wall, in places spilling through into the house itself.

The construction is simple, made from four kind-of woven wood walls and kept cool by the thick thatch roof. There are just two rooms; the main room and an open topped bathroom, divided by a hardwood board hinged on thick twine and latched using a leather belt with the buckle facing inwards. Between the inside and the scorched grass outside was some sort of broken door, like a segment of wall but more loose.

The double mattress on the floor made the main space into a bedroom, it looked like it was wet once but had been air dried since. A single bulb hung from the central beam by a length of grey cable that looped in and out of the bare bamboo supports and down to the light switch – which was springing inches from the doorframe on its exposed wiring.

The usable floor space was a foot wide slice down the edge of the bed where the wall very almost reached the floor – there were a handful of cable-ties and a stained bamboo bong in the far corner, but aside from this, the place was empty.

The simplicity was so refreshing, just throwing my mind back to the white walled grey seat life over the ocean gave me a bout of panic and anxiety. Through abandonment the wooden plank flooring had acquired a lot of sand, blown in presumably through the patchy walls, I sat on my mattress and drew in it with my toes. Hours passed without a worry in the world.

December 7ᵗʰ
There was a huge cockroach in the bathroom this morning. I thought to myself, 'Wow that is the biggest insect I've ever seen.'

I bought a dirt-cheap bottle of that green Fairy brand dish washing liquid. It will also have to act as body wash and shampoo for the time being.

I opened the bathroom door to find a huge spider with half of the cockroach in its chompers, I decided I'm okay with spiders if they eat bugs.

I went to teach Noi some English; Nim had given us some picture books to work through but most of the time we just point at things we can see from where we are sitting. Dow has been teaching me a bit of Thai, but I think I pick up more from Noi.

Came back from lessons to find my spider has been replaced by a big, fat, very green, lizard. It was sitting on the back of the toilet bucket chewing something. I think I know what happened to the spider.

I also think I'm going to keep away from this food chain demonstration that's taking place in my bathroom.

Final update on the circle of life: Lizard is gone, keeping my eye out for the terrifying reason why.

Lemon – scene 4

'Look at these snow dogs,' Lemon had been staring transfixed at the tightly wrapped people living in the coldest parts of my globe. 'Six of them and only one of the people!' She was always pointing out small peculiarities; I think soon she will know more about the people than I do.

'You think the dogs are their pets?' I asked only to humour her. I knew the answer – the dogs were their cars. I zoomed into her line of sight and sure enough there were two lines of dogs pulling one human on a sledge.

She looked to me with an eye closing slightly as she pushed a suppressed smile into her cheek, I knew this meant she was about to say something she thought was funny. 'Maybe we got it wrong,' she said, holding on tightly to her almost straight face, 'maybe these dogs just take a packed lunch with them everywhere they go and when they are hungry they all turn around and ...' She let the grin escape in tandem with a loud growling noise and curled her hands into makeshift claws.

It was funny, in a way. Maybe she liked jokes about a human being torn apart by six dogs. I should try one like this and maybe she will like it too. 'Sometimes the tigers eat people.' Wait, that wasn't funny! Why did I say that?

She looked at me, expressionless, then said, 'Sometimes they eat the tigers so ...'

'They eat all the animals!' It spilled out of my mouth, were we having an argument, or were we both agreeing a lot? What was even happening here?

'Not all of them,' Lemon pointed out, then clarified, 'They don't eat all of the animals, not, they don't all eat animals.'

She was wrong on both counts, some of the people would eat anything, and some wouldn't eat any animals at all. It was as if what was acceptable to eat reached new standards as the people change with time, but the people in some places took a little longer. In their earliest times the first people ate everything from worms to wolves to each other. Now the people in one area don't like it when another area eats the dogs, because they themselves don't eat the dogs anymore. There are even people who don't like it that others eat the cows because they don't eat the cows now. It just kept going around like that.

I think in time the people who eat the dogs will also change, but how the two groups see each other will stay the same because by this time the others won't even be eating the cows anymore. It's like they all follow the same path, but some are years behind or ahead.

I thought about how I would explain this to Lemon, but things would often disorganise themselves between my thoughts and my words. It all went sideways and I panicked posing a new question, 'What's your favourite colour?' mostly by mistake.

'Yellow,' she replied, her brow furrowed in a humorously discombobulated sort of way, 'for obvious reasons.'

'What would happen?' she inquired again.

I really like it when she needed an explanation. Lemon was such a fast learner that already she was often the one explaining to me what was happening.

'Well it's just their brains,' I began, 'they make themselves think they expected something to happen, after it's happened.' Time with Lemon was like something I had never experienced, to be able to talk to someone so freely and easily was a level of comfort I thought I would never achieve.

'I can show you,' I picked up a waxy leaf and started moving it towards the earth.

'Don't hurt them!'

'I would never,' I assured her, briefly picturing the flood and that one time I lost a city in the ocean. 'I'll only hide the moon, just for a second.'

'Will they be scared?' she looked concerned.

'That's the thing, when it happens they first see it and right away they will fill in the part that they didn't understand,' I tried to be more clear with a quick reword, 'So the moon will vanish and their minds will immediately find a reason.'

'They will invent something so they are not so scared?'

'Right, but what's really more amazing than that, is the things they can come up with,' I had a feeling she was going to find this hard to understand. 'Some of them will think their moon was hidden or blocked by something, but some will actually convince themselves that they knew it was going to happen all along and it's not strange at all.'

'They think it's normal when the moon disappears?' Her head tilted to one side in disbelief. 'Really? Actually?'

'Well yes ...' I tried one more time, it was worth it; she had to know this. 'They need to invent a reason they can understand. They need it so much so that a lot of them will actually create a memory of knowing the moon will vanish and this memory will fit into their mind in a slot before it happened.'

'So they will never know they were confused?' Lemon added to my point to show she understood. 'That's incredible, and they do this a lot?'

'They do it a lot, for a lot of things.' I searched for an example but another thought crossed into my mouth, 'That is, when they don't just guess correctly.'

'Sometimes they know it's you, like they know they were made?' A tone of excitement tinged the final note of her question.

I reached down and slid the leaf under the moon and out the other side. The people below understood this in whichever way they needed to. 'I didn't say that,' I told her, 'I said that sometimes they guess.'

Chapter 10 - the moment you forget

December 10th

I bought some candles, thankfully Thailand is very cheap. Now I can use the bathroom at night. What an amazing way of life, to swim in crystal clear waters and watch the world's best sunsets for about 39 cents a day. I had finally found proof that you didn't need to save, or plan, or play it safe – you just need to find out what you need to be happy and simply remove everything else – and if it all went wrong, anyone can live on coconuts and tap water.

There was a lunar eclipse tonight. I was with Dow and her family when it happened and as it turns out Thai people are really superstitious. Dow showed me one of the many tattoos she has; this one was of a monster eating a pancake. She told me it was a demon eating the moon and that many Thai people believe that one day this will happen and the demon will never give the moon back.

A lot of people freaked out at the eclipse, so much so that I found myself wondering if just this time, maybe, the moon wouldn't come back straight away. Then of course it did come back, mostly because it was the moon being shadowed by the earth and it wasn't being eaten by a demon.

I told Dow I was glad the demon gave the moon back. She told me to have some respect for people's beliefs - but I think she was joking.

December 14th

Tonight I went to the beach party with a bunch of lady-boys.

Dow's good friends also happen to be transgender workers in the island's tiny red light district. They were a lot of fun but it got a bit crazy towards the end. A few things I learned:

- Lady-boys really prefer to be called girls.

- They can drink like pirates.

- Their massage shop is also a brothel.

- Sometimes they don't tell guys they are Trans.

I asked Nok, one of the girls, why she didn't mention her sex change up-front. She grabbed her package and reassured me, 'They know soon enough.'

After a lot of whisky we went to the beach. It's an impressive sight; fire shows, laser lights, different music in every bar and a lot of distracting bodies.

The massage shop girls went, in their own words, 'fishing for cock.' This was pretty much exactly what it sounded like and I watched as they cast themselves out into the drunken souls of the beach party and reeled back once they had hooked something. It didn't take long for them to lead a guy up the beach road towards the shop. Some came back before two songs had played out, maybe they were turned off by their penis surprise, most didn't come back for a half hour. I gawked at the machine that was their nightly fishing trip. It was a fast process, gutting out the pockets, catch and release.

Things were great. The people were amazing. The music, the scene, the energy was overwhelming. Then things turned nasty.

December 14th   23:44

The moment you forget is a blank second before a shock. Somebody screamed. Terror. The tone of this scream came like a stone dropping into the sea of skin; the ripple consisted of turning heads.

Panicked and desperate, falling both arms first, she piled into the sand. Two white half-moons as ruby red split her face from her hairline to her lower lip.

The whites of eyes passed mine as she searched for a saviour, standing then stumbling to the ground. A green glass bottle spun out of the dark, missing her head and digging into the sand, its path dividing the crowd and framing three men in the opening between the street and beach.

In the semi-silhouettes, the outline of one was illuminated with a baseball bat held high above his head. The two on each side presenting a front of an imminent attack - in the seconds it took me to understand what was happening - the tide of party animals that lapped up the sides of the scene started to surge back in an attempt to close the gap and block the attack.

There is a flicker of shame; I'm still rooted to the spot and my grandfather had told me to never be an onlooker, to either help or leave. The shouts of the attackers still stood out over the commotion, their deranged anger didn't need a translator.

The crowd, brave from drink and numbers, swarmed back around the bleeding girl, veiling her in commotion and chaos.

The shamefully one-sided attack of three men going after a lone girl seemed to have been overcome and the party people stood tall - right up until two bullets were let loose into the sky. It happened fast, the shockwave from these two shots brought people to their knees, an instinctive reflex. Their bravado shrunk back as fast as it had rose revealing nothing but some blood on the sand.

The helping hands had successfully fed the girl through the throng of onlookers to a safe space and the left hand man, with his pistol raised towards the sky, slowly lowered it in an arc aiming across the crowd before realising his situation and turning away. Their gold necklaces caught the moon and the men swaggered back up the street.

Chapter 11 – slack tide

Some say to have nothing is to have nothing to lose, a quote for the miserable. As I reached the beach, with all traces of last night swept clean by the coastal winds, the three silhouettes stuck in my mind not just because of what they had done, but what they had taken from me.

They were the first stain on my paradise and what this island meant to me was more than an escape from the western world. The land of smiles had stuck to its reputation, the magic and the warmth not only of the soft Thai sun and the roaring campfire but the people, all of the people. Now in this scene there was a small crack and somehow it bothered me more than the shattered view I held of the world beyond that fine line where the earth curved out of view.

I had passed some of the same faces from the night before, treating this day as any other because for them it was an incident to add to a passing experience, but for me this was a chip in the bedrock of a new idea, a new way to think and breathe; a place to be carefree. I sat in my usual spot and stared out to sea.

It was the moment that sailors call a 'slack tide' – the turning point between rising and falling when the sea is neither giving nor taking the land. A standstill as boats bob closer to their buoy lines and the ropes dip under lack of tension, revolving with the natural swell of outside influence.

What's this? A crab. Perched on a flip-flop. The foam base was lifting and falling with each ripple in the lapping tide as it touched and retreated, the shoe itself was on its own fine line - right on the edge of being taken by the turn of the tide or left to curl up in the hot sun.

At first glance I thought little of it, but as I watched this purple pattern flip-flop and its passenger lifting from, and settling back into the sand, the crab crouched all eight legs on deck and I wondered if it had a more adventurous reason than a good supply of shoe algae.

If only the crab knew that the outcome of the potential voyage was solely dictated by the pull of the moon, that distant powerful orb that hauled the seas up the shores, drew the howl out of the lone wolf and had found itself as a god throughout history. The passing gravity of this mystical magica... oh!

A passing long-tail boat had pushed an extra-large ripple inland and ever so softly broke contact between the crab's vessel and dry land. Well, so much for the sole power of the moon. Anyway, the crab didn't react to this. It barely even moved as the inches between sand and shoe increased, drawing it away on the newly receding waterline and further from the beach.

I looked at the crab and then far across the ocean, a shimmering gold danced across the surface letting the sun's rays play from the shore right into the horizon, and highlighting nothing but open water. No distant shore, neither a lone standing rock, not even a cloud.

So where are you going little crab?

The crab – episode 1

He watched the human carefully, feeling like he was being judged. 'Like you're so special with your four stalks and twenty eyes, half the time the lower ten can't see for all the sand they've got stuck to them! If that idiot picks up my boat and puts me back on dry land, I vow I'll pinch him! You know! I'm a crab, I can swim, so don't save me!' This would be his second attempt at escape and this time it would be successful.

He reeled off a final speech in his head 'So goodbye island of birds with long beaks, goodbye beach of a million seafood barbeques and goodbye to the harbour full of fishing boats – and good riddance.'

A wave took charge of the moment and pulled the boat a little further from the shore, 'Well, shit, here I go – just as long as I don't float straight into that boat's propeller ...' The crab held still, so the human didn't think he was panicking and try to help out, and watched the space between foam and sand stretch a little farther.

He had just settled in for a relaxing float out to sea when a shadow passed between him and the sun, 'Whoa, what was that! A bird?' Hitting the deck he looked up to see just a boat mast passing by, but the scare was enough to prompt being a bit more careful and the crab moved to hang out on the sole until he was out of the thick of it. 'Blub!'

This was the last we saw of him for quite some time.

Chapter 12 - research

December 18th

Found a beach bar with a Wi-Fi connection I can connect to from my hut. The internet here is quite censored. It seems that a lot of political blogs, news websites and porn sites trigger a green 'blocked website' warning. I'm not really interested in politics and news at this time of day.

It took a few minutes to work out how to get around the third. For those who might be interested, the system seems to work out a keyword recognition scheme. Too many sexual references in the English and, presumably, Thai language automatically blocks the page. Changing the .com to .es on any multilingual website will load the text in Spanish, eliminating the problem and accessing the page.

In another fascinating revelation, each country's version of the same pornographic website has a completely different 'most viewed' or 'most popular' section. You learn something new every day. The Germans seem to use a lot of equipment, whereas the British .co.uk version just uses a lot of people. Sweden seemed quite pleasant at first glance and .it for Italy showed some vast age differences – food for thought.

Note to self: when in uncensored country try image searching a translation of the same word in the local language using that countries version of Google, then compare top viewed results. For research purposes.

Another note to self: Stop searching weird stuff on the Wi-Fi I borrowed an hour ago.

Opened Facebook for a bit. Daryl Daniels and his girlfriend are having a baby. Well, I think that's what they mean when they say, 'Our two has become three!' and I assume they aren't just boasting about group sex.

Went back to research. Who even writes in the comments section on a porn video? What sort of person is sitting there and thinking, 'Oh hey, I'll share my opinion with other guys who are holding their cocks.'

This could be a great way to learn Spanish.

Chapter 13 – 'The beach campfire' - a wildlife documentary [read in a posh-British old-man voice]

Here we are in South-East Asia, a humid wasteland in the heart of the tropics. Each week upwards of ten-thousand twenty-somethings embark on an almost tribal and highly spiritual migration to this distant and mystical land.

We focus in on one beachfront campfire in a typical hotspot where these travellers are often known to gather. The glowing embers act in much the same way as a fallen elephant carcass would in the desolate African Serengeti, attracting a vast but kindred range of sub-species to its allure.

Here we can see the early arrival of a humble backpacker attracted by the promise of a cheap night, this backpacker has been on the road for many months. His aim, of course, is to follow his heart as far as he can before the last few digits of his bank account run dry. The backpacker is brave and confident in the vicinity of any campfire as he knows that his people are the starters of campfires and he would be amongst friends here.

As ritual dictates, on his approach to the circle the backpacker must present two or more alcoholic beverages held in plain view of the group, these are not intended as an offering but as a signal to the residents that he would indeed be consuming his own beverages and not drinking from the metaphorical watering hole. This solo traveller is much versed in such protocol and as the minimart is the backpackers favourite bar he has produced not two but four cans of cheap lager as a guarantee of self-sufficiency.

The newcomer recites a set script acted out by generations before him, the do-si-do of 'where are you from?' - with a complicated answer. Where have you been? - followed by a list commonly shared by most listeners. This time the standard 'favourite place' question has been brought to a halt by a gaggle of giggles making their way down the beach, the noisiest of all the long-term travellers, a huddle of four young gap-packers relishing their year long 'self discovery tour' around South-East Asia, a rite of passage known only as 'The Gap Year'.

Known to stick with the herd, the common gap-packer is often wary in the presence of newcomers, protecting one another from making bad decisions. This pack mentality is strong but often shows weakness in the face of a member of the opposite sex who has chosen to travel with a guitar, lulling the youngsters into a false sense of security with renditions of Wonderwall.

There was no doubt these two subspecies would make a social connection as they all find themselves on a very similar path. Some may call it simply 'the South-East Asia circuit' but, for this mix in particular, that brand would challenge the feeling of independent travel that they have carefully cultivated. Nevertheless the circuit, in general, goes something like this: Thailand, Khao San, elephants, tattoos, full moon party, Laos, Vang Vieng (tubing), friendship bracelets, Cambodia, Angkor Wat, Sihanoukville, MDMA, Koh Rong, sunsets, cocktails, Instagram, Vietnam, rented scooter, hospital, anonymous sex, tearful goodbyes, pinkie promises, cheap t-shirts, antibiotics and missing flip-flops.

In the mid distance an unruly Brit shouts at the moon. 'Fuck yeeeeeah Thailand!' echoes from deep inside his bare vibrating stomach, bouncing from the cliffs that glow orange in the firelight. Drunk level: Henry 8th, he has a bare confidence rarely presented by his sober self.

But wait, what's this? A potential suitor, or a challenger, has approached the vicinity, only time will tell what happens next. As the space closes between the shirtless duo, two sets of arms fly open. It's a hug! Wait no, just a chest bump. The newcomer is a friend and in quite a display of camaraderie they splat together in a touching moment.

With Christmas less than a week away a similar collection of travellers also frequent the circuit, but not for the long haul, no. Commonly referred to as a 'Flashpackers' by anyone but themselves, the flashpackers take a direct flight to Asia on the first day of their holiday in the knowledge that their time is limited, what with their careers and responsibilities. The Flashpacker often travels alone adorning themselves with much the same attire as the Backpacker. This camouflage, although effective, can often be betrayed by the flashpackers lust for all things 'now' – the newest gadgets and the best brands hide amongst their Bob Marley pants, and as the day draws to an end they will be retiring to a private room, as opposed to the backpackers eighteen-bed corridor with things that scuttle and bite in the night.

Each of the many types of travellers who find themselves wandering the vast South-East Asian 'wilderness' hold one thing in common, however, the memento of each journey, which hangs around the necks of some and rattles upon the wrists of others.

The 'Asia beer brand' tank top is a must have for any drunken Welshman - and for the self-respecting hippie, maybe a nice stone or something.

But one of the most common souvenirs to be taken home with you from this beautiful metropolis is shared by each and every sub species of traveller, but none so much as the topless Scandinavian. In Thailand we would call it a 'roi sak' – in London it's a tattoo - innit!

Chapter 14 – roi sak

December 19th

Christmas is coming, apparently - it definitely didn't feel that way. The sun was baking into my shoulders so I chose a refuge, the pull-out shelter outside one of the islands traditional stick-and-poke tattoo shops gave shade for people looking at the book of quotes and designs.

There was Beth doing just that. I didn't know her name until she turned to me presenting herself Brazilian flag bikini top first and said, 'Hi. Beth,' holding a hand out.

I was like 'Hi.'

'Sooooo ummmm I'm thinking something along these lines,' Beth told me, out of the blue, running a finger under seven or eight drawings that looked like the recycling logo.

Something I have recently realised about travellers, all the types, with Beth included, was that you don't often have a choice when it comes to hearing their newfound life philosophies; it's just part of the introduction somehow. 'I don't believe in God, I believe in Karma,' had come up in the first five minutes.

'That's cool,' I said.

Beth was one of those people that nod when they make a point and if you don't nod as well she feels the need to explain. I didn't know this at first so, 'Karma, when you do good things and good things will come to you,' was explained to me like I was five. I was thinking about something else for several seconds until she said, 'That's the basis for my tattoo, this is why I came to you ...'

Nonplussed I chose to say, 'Okay,' and waited to see where this was going.

'Soooo,' she said again, 'something like one of these,' she indicated to the page once more, 'but better. Sorry if they're ones that you drew.'

Well, now I could guess that Beth wrongfully thought I worked here, but instead of correcting her I chose to say 'okay' again. Maybe I should say something more interesting, I chose another uninteresting solitary word 'Where?'

It turns out that this was a good question when Beth spun back around and pulled the back of her Bikini halfway down. 'Aha!' I exclaimed noncommittally.

By now I wasn't sure how to tell her I was just hanging around saying 'okay' to stuff so we went through the designs, I figured 'in for a penny in for a pound' still unsure why I was in for the penny in the first place. Saying things like 'which one do you like most' and 'but maybe with a bit of this one mixed in with it' was a great way to spend more time in the shade and at around waist height.

Beth has solidly linked the whole 'reduce, reuse, recycle' triangle made of arrows to her love of karma, and that was fine I guess. Saying 'okay' and 'cool' got less nonchalant when she asked me where she could sit while I drew it up for her. Best answer - 'Anywhere.'

There were pens everywhere - and some paper, leftover from cut-out transfers I guess, so I drew some sort of nice circle of arrows and shrugged. She asked me if I liked it, which I did, it was kind-of a nice circle of arrows and I had managed to drop the triangle shape you see on trash cans.

What do you say to people thinking of getting tattoos when you're in too deep to explain that you're an idiot, there are a lot of options but I went with a friendly, 'You should take a walk around and think about it.'

'Will you still be working at half past nine?'

Oh, here we go, we're about to cross the line between non-truths and lies. 'Yes,' I said, line equals crossed.

So the goodbye hug was squishy and now I was just standing there, a little confused why I was even inside the shop.

'She friend you?' The only tattoo artist in the shop, who I thought wasn't paying attention, was now just sitting there looking up at me.

'Maybe.' What a stupid answer. Think of something else quickly, 'Ummm, I was just helping her to pick a design.'

'She come back, mai?' he asked, this guy looked a lot like a pirate.

'Yes, she will come back at nine thirty,' I told him, preparing to leave.

'You stay okay, take Chang beer, at nine thirty she take tattoo and I give you commission,' his smile was like a split in a rubber boot. The gold hanging from him was somehow less busy than his tattoo-sheathed skin.

'I have to eat something first,' I told him.

'Eat Chang beer Mr ...?' the guy asked.

'Clem,' I told him, holding out a hand.

'Bua,' said Bua, shaking it. Rings clicked together in my palm. 'She have tattoo, Kim have percent ten,' held up both hands fingers stretched.

I decided not to tell Bua that I had met Beth half way inside the door already, and joined him for a Chang beer before finishing some Papaya salad a French girl left half-eaten on the worktop.

December 19th one minute early

The numbers said 20:29.

'This is Clem, he draws the tattoos here,' Beth threw a hand from the three other girls who had followed her into the shop, and motioned towards me. By now my silence means I'm either officially lying or officially drawing tattoos.

Enter Bua, stage right, 'Him Kim,' thanks Bua. 'Kim need Bua, Kim ask Bua, okay,' he said. Actually that could be useful.

'First question!' bounced the brunette, 'does it hurt?'

I could answer that one, 'Yes,' then soften it, 'a bit.'

'Not much, much pain machine tattoo,' Bua chimed from the background. Okay check, now I know something at least.

Beth stepped back in, 'I meant to ask how long will it be until I can go in the sea again?'

'Ummm ..'

'Tattoo today, water same time tomorrow,' Bua shot me a smile, 'not like machine.'

Another one of Beth's friends spoke up, 'So it's not really like a normal tattoo then, the bamboo style?'

'It's the same, it's just a different way of getting the ink under the skin,' Beth assured her, I guess she knew more about it than me, 'don't worry, it takes a little longer, but it's not as painful.'

'Oh,' she popped back in line with the others, and then hopped forward again to ask me, 'so how exactly does it work?'

Bua to the rescue, thank Buddha. 'It just like this,' he said, holding up a foot long thin piece of stripped bamboo, 'Needle end of bamboo take ink and Bua put the ink into the skin like this,' he leant the stick over his thumb and forefinger and holding the butt end with the same fingers on his other hand he pulsated the rod back and forth, 'bamboo tattoo very good, good Thai style kaap,' he assured.

Just like that, everyone was in. All four of them, so as Bua transferred my last sketch onto Beth's butt, I got to drawing something like what they were describing, that would become the permanent cultural memento of this particular trip.

I drew paw prints up a wrist, because she loves dogs so much! A copy of a traditional Thai protection symbol was an easy one to pass over to Bua and the birth dates of the last girl's family transferred easily onto the inside the upper arm. It was fun, helping people with the designs, checking up on them as they were inked and sharing a shot with them when all was done.

After the last shot was down and I made promises to meet them somewhere later, Bua turned to me. Now that was a happy guy.

Two of the tattoos were three thousand baht and the other two were for two thousand. 'Mr Kim keep,' he handed me a thousand baht note, 'Bua give Kim for all tattoo Kim help.'

This was great news, I hadn't really expected to get paid for all four of the designs. 'You happy, me happy Kim,' he beamed. 'What time Kim come tomorrow?'

'In ... the morning?' I ventured a guess.

'In the morning Kim!' Bua showed me a thumbs up.

I'm not completely sure how today happened.

'Hey, you.' She was here and she was wearing a red hat.

'Why are you wearing a hat?'

'Oh I don't know, I just felt like throwing it on.'

She *just felt* like throwing a red hat on her head? But why? I should ask, this the sort of thing I should ask about.

'So, you're ready?' She stepped to the globe. Lemon gracefully folded herself onto the balls of her feet and then popped forward onto her knees. She adjusted her hat a little.

'Why did you throw it on your head?' I said it carefully, but it was a valid question.

'What?'

'The red ...'

'Oh, for goodness sake, I have a red hat, it's on my head,' she looked at my face, 'And now I don't!' She whipped it off with a flourish and placed it beside her with a smile and a half shake of her head.

I was glad. Who just throws something so big and red on their head without a valid reason?

'Shall we?' she was looked at me with a grin, one hand half-way to the sheet.

'Oh, right.' What was wrong with me? I said yes, but by the time I reached out she was already moving the sheet, so I took my corner and lifted with Lemon.

After catching up with the snow dogs and following a train from London to Southampton, Lemon placed both hands in the grass, lowering her body until her cheek was almost to the ground. Her behind was up in the air, I looked, then looked away. She didn't see what I had done. 'What are you doing?' I asked her, my eyes carefully averted.

'I'm looking for your island.' The words came out funny with her face pressed to the ground.

'I can just ...' I moved to turn the world. I wanted her off the ground and with her behind rested on her heels rather than up in the air.

'No!' She looked down and caught my eye, well I guess she actually looked kind-of sideways-up as her face was flat to the grass. 'I don't like it when you do that!'

'I told you it doesn't hurt them.'

She lifted her head up from under the globe. 'It does something to them,' she retorted. She was right; a turn in the world can shorten a day a little, or alter the weather. I told her this. She replied, 'Well, they don't like it!'

'They don't know!' I said, 'They just correct their mind.' I had explained all this before, 'They use phrases like 'time flies' or 'that was a long day,' but they don't really think ...'

'Just stop it okay!' Lemon pushed herself up from the ground and looked at me reproachfully. 'It's just not fair, just because they don't realise what you're doing doesn't make it a nice thing to do.'

I nodded, not because I agreed as much as because that hot spreading sensation was back. I hadn't felt uncomfortable around Lemon since I had to pretend that the island was my favourite place. My eyes moistened a little and I knew I had to do something to distract myself so I put my face in the grass.

'I found it!' I prematurely pointed as I frantically scanned the coast of Thailand.

'Hello!' Her face was right beside mine, smiling. 'Oh yes, here we are.' I followed her gaze, and there it was again. Phew.

It was a dream really, lying in the cold grass with Lemon, close but not touching, both concentrating on something else. The people on the island were celebrating their nightly ritual where they met on the shoreline and watched the sun go to India.

'Did you ever think, for your people,' her voice sounded less inquisitive and more like when someone is musing out loud to themselves, 'that every night they watch this sunset, but really, there's only ever been one sunset, it just goes around and around.'

She is either smart or dumb, I can't work it out.

The crab – episode 2

It had been days since the crab had seen the comfort of sand passing below the flip-flop with that chain-link effect from the sun shining through the surface of the sea. He had felt a little unsure then, as he squinted through the glare at the bottom feeders becoming sparser and a little further away. This baseless fear had become reality as the sandbank dropped out from below him, the safety net of shallow water had turned from crystal clear, to a blue-haze and finally to black.

As he left the tip of the island the sea became ocean and the sun that once lit up the sand now shone lances through the depths as it petered out into the darkness. A squad of squids passed ghostly through the growing depth, barely illuminated by the glow, and as the sun slowly dropped below the horizon, even that security of a few extra metres of warning left with it.

He watched as the clouds piled to one side of the jungle peak, a gathered collection of oranges and reds, before they took on the darkness of the water just centimetres to each side of him. A ripple caught the edge of the flip-flop; caused by water movement, not movement in the water, he told himself. The idea of what else might be out there with him hadn't crossed his mind until now. The world was his to claim and this ship was his vessel to claim it. He was sure of this, but as he recalled some of the fleshy shapes that had washed up on the island's shore, the flip-flop suddenly started to feel a little thin.

But this was it, right? The point of the unknown - and of no return. This was what he had been searching for - of course it would inspire fears, of course it would be bleak sometimes. He stared to the hunched figure of the island, two mountains on either end jutting like the folded legs of a crouching insect. It was only visible now by the stars it blocked from sight.

'Who drew them then?'

'The people did,' I told her, 'Well, not the people who are here now, the ones that came before them.'

'Why?'

'I don't know,' I admitted. 'Maybe so people know where in the world they are.'

'It's more than that though,' Lemon traced her finger between Sweden and Norway, a line that was vaguely marked by sign posts and a track cut into the forest. 'This one isn't guarded at all.'

Lemon had been watching the dividing line between Myanmar and Thailand after spotting road blocks just north of the island. I had told her the people drew lines so they can decide who can cross them and who must stay on the other side but she was struggling to see why. Honestly it didn't make sense to me either.

She looked back to the lines around Thailand; every road had a place where the people had to stop and pay money before they continued into the country. If you looked closely at the jungle sometimes you could find people crossing without stopping. They walked for weeks to stay away from the blocked part of the road and sometimes they didn't come out of the other side at all.

'Look at this dead girl.' Lemon pointed out a huddled figure slumped mid-way between the two countries. 'Isn't that the saddest thing?'

'Please don't.' I'd hoped she wouldn't see these things, at a glance you could see that the people could be cruel but I didn't want her to know how much pain was really down there. After all, everything that happened, good and bad, was put, sort-of, into motion by me. I had once thought about shaking the globe and ending it all; this was after watching a group of men hurting a family in Johannesburg, but now Lemon had come along and made me focus on the beauty that existed in my small world.

I had to clear the silence, what were we talking about? I started my best explanation with one word, 'Berries.'

'Berries?' she looked up at me questioningly.

'Berries is how they started,' I regained control of the conversation and drew it away from dead girls in jungle crossings, 'the divides between the countries I mean, berries are what started it, pretty much.'

'How did berries start them?' a small crease furrowed into the middle of her brow.

I hoped for the best that this would come out well, recalling some of the first people I had ever tried out. 'So it happened somewhere around here I think,' I reached out and drew a vague circle around Africa, 'back when there weren't so many people, just a few small groups that mostly ate wild fruit to stay alive.'

Lemon raised her eyebrows, a soundless challenge to my facts.

'Well they didn't know they could eat the animals, and they didn't understand that you can grow the plants from seeds, so they just ate what they could find. There was this one guy who was eating berries ...'

'Okay, sure,' she still looked sceptical.

'And so one day he went to eat and saw another man eating the berries. He knew that there weren't many berries left and he knew when they were all gone he would have to walk a long way to find more berries, so he chased the other man away.'

'So he decided the berries were only for him?' Lemon carried my story along, 'But the other man would just come back later and eat them all.'

'Right.' I told her, 'The first man knew that now he had to protect his berries, so he relocated his entire family to where the berries were so he could be there all the time. To be sure they were safe, he made a wall of sticks and stones around his family and the bushes to show the other man that these were his berries.'

'So he made a border?' Lemon made an easy conclusion.

'Well he made a pile of stones.' I could have just agreed and stopped there, but there was more to it than that, now I wanted to tell her what I'd seen. 'His son grew up believing that whatever was inside the wall belonged to his family, maybe he even built the wall a little further out himself - to claim some orange trees or something.'

'And that man's son would think the same, and do the same?' Lemon shrugged and smiled with her mouth, but not her eyes. 'It's inherited greed?'

'Sure, so then millions of their years later, the son of the same family is standing on a stage giving a long speech about the land inside this very long wall. He talks about restricting who can cross the wall and how much people have to pay if they want to come in. He tells the people that the berries are their property and they must protect them with their life and he locks people in boxes if they stay inside the wall longer than the time that they paid for ...'

'But they know that someone just built a wall around the berries right?'

'I'm sure they do, but they don't think about it that way,' I was getting out of my depth here answering these questions, I tried to finish up, 'It's just what they do.'

'But the people on this side of the border are hungry and sick and some of them on the other side are so fat, why don't they share the food with ...' She had started on a train of thought I didn't know how to answer.

'I really don't know.' I cut her off, 'They must have a reason, maybe they don't care about the hungry people.'

'That can't be true?'

She was right, something was very wrong here.

Chapter 15 - worshipping the storm

December 20th

'Don't do it!' a voice like soup came through the door, I was repositioning the first few lines of a song up the underside of the guy's forearm. Of course I looked up. 'You'll regret it one day!' the same voice, thick through half a slice of pizza. I cocked my head in the direction of the overweight girl feeding herself in the middle of the road. 'You're ruining your body' she added.

Oh, irony. She added cheese to her midsection which escaped the bikini strap like a tree growing too close to a fence.

'Jah, I don't think I am ze one who need to worry,' the German in my chair muttered under his breath.

This was something that happened daily, a tattoo is permanent but so is death by heart disease so this one was easy to laugh off. Even though everyone had the right to make their own choices, I was a big fan of making people take a half day to decide, or sober up.

So I found my level of comfort when it came to drawing on people, dissuading them from 'tattoos of passion' or anything around the face and hands.

Every day was great, I spent some time with Dow, some time with Noi and the rest of the time in the shop with Bua.

'Kim?'

'Kaap,' I was saying things in Thai and getting them wrong a lot.

'Have working visa, mai?'

'Umm no,' I told him, 'I didn't think about it.'

'Not a problem Kim, can work no problem, Bua speak to big boss for you okay?'

Okay, so there was a boss. I had just assumed that Bua was running the shop for himself. I told him, 'I need to go to the border to get a new visa soon, they gave me one month when I arrived.'

Bua looked thoughtful, 'Kim, next two week Christmas and your New Year very busy, Bua need Kim,' then added, 'Go now not late.'

'My visa will finish on the new year,' I told him

'Okay Kim, have money, mai? Go now better.'

He had a good point, everyone said it would get much busier around the holidays, so I got down to planning my visa run to the Malaysian border.

December 21st

I was in the world of the numbers once more.

6:30am   cough up last night, bucket shower, eat rice.

7:30am   board the boat to the mainland, not a great feeling.

9:30am   catch shuttle to the nearest town, love aircon; hate hangover.

9:55am   rushed to the long-haul bus to Hat-Yai, border crossing city.

14:00   arrive in Hat-Yai, wait for the next bus in the direction of Kuala Lumpur.

17:00 the bus drops all passengers at the Thai side of the Bukit Kayu border crossing, with the intention of collecting them on the Malaysian side of the customs barrier. Of course I wouldn't be boarding again because once I had left I would be doubling back into Thailand on foot.

17:20 stamp out of Thailand (ten days early) walk about 100 meters.

17:30 stamp into Malaysia, no problems, then do a U-turn

17:35 stamp back out of Malaysia, walk back along the same 100 metre road

17:45 stamp back into Thailand, no problems there.

18:10 board the first bus destined for Phuket and jump off as close to the island crossing as possible.

Sleep anywhere, eat anything, take a motorbike taxi to the fishing port and step back onto the island by midday, eat with Bua, drink with friends, sleep with strangers.

Christmas Eve

I walked a little faster as the sky shifted gears, from pouring to forcibly kicking raindrops out of the night. At a time like this I get an amazing feeling, like a splice between mind and body. I have always loved it there, that state of being where your body and brain are on a separate plane. It can come mid-way through a run or in the cycle of a repetitive task. When your mind jumps, fights and takes flight. Words can do this for you, when you're completely lost in the lyrics and acting out the scene, when you're jogging or sawing wood - your mind is having an incredibly different experience to your physical self. If you don't know what I mean, I hope you do one day.

I was wading now in a shin-deep rushing slush of I-don't-know-what knocking past my ankles and bare feet. The sandals had been a drawback to who I wanted to be, so I lost them. A lump in my throat blocked the howl to the moon that swelled in my lungs, all this from the personal realisation that comes with the moment.

That's right, when you zoom out and see yourself, standing there mid-way through your life, you see yourself for who you are. For so many of us this feeling will be heavy, overburdened, a focus on the mistakes and regrets, the feel of the weight of the rain and the sharp of the grit - this is their life.

If you're in the right place and you brought yourself there, the noise will be incredible. You see all you can be, rife with opportunities, possibilities, pictures of heroism and ecstasy swimming in your mind. In this second I am so far from being an insignificant blur behind sheets of monsoon rain, hitting so fast that deafening waterfalls thunder off the flat tin roofs to either side. More blissfully disconnected than enlightened I drifted in the love of life. The storm was determined to distract me as those clouds kicked the bass drum and the street turned white; far from distracting, exhilarating! The rain all came down at once, ten seconds of white noise receded to reveal the final piece I needed to complete this high. Music.

Deep long bass punctuated the roar of falling water. I felt sick with it, completely delirious with the power of man and nature. Flash. I made up my mind; this was me now, who I am. Flash! Flash! The strobe of lightning silhouetted a scene. Ahead, what were before, indecipherable shadows in the storm, became human forms. Standing in the centre of street, with their arms in the air, they were right at the source of the beat. Dancing? No. Worshipping the storm. Stomping it out in the pouring rain.

I took a sip, what were they drinking? It tasted like rocket fuel. Ten straws in four colours shoved under my nose by a dripping blonde in a T-shirt and bikini bottoms. A sodden Swedish flag hung vertical in line with the torrent from above, the lights changed to nobody's tune.

Time passed in the outside world. Trains arrived on time, deals were sealed. Kisses were missed and plates were dropped. I remember nothing.

December 25th
I can hear myself blink.

Found a hole in my wall big enough to pee through, mostly, and then decided to go back to sleep, which went okay but I can hear monkeys jumping on the roof. I don't even know if I like monkeys anymore, I always thought I did, but now I'm on the fence.

I'm still too hung-over to shout. They are tearing at the straw on the roof. I can hear it snap. I saw some little macaques gang-rushing a bakery somewhere near the Malay border – what was funny then is less funny now.

I had been watching my eyelids for half an hour before little brown monkey fingers came through the straw! Is this what happens when I'm not at home? I wanted to pull a monkey finger to see what happened but it felt a bit mean and who knows if that monkey was the next up on the 'cockroach, spider, lizard' food chain. I wouldn't want it to become 'cockroach, spider, lizard, monkey, Clem... tiger maybe?' – Whatever the hierarchy I'm going to keep out of it.

Do monkeys eat meat? I guess they grab stuff, maybe it just grabbed the lizard and threw it somewhere. The main problem with obsessing over monkeys for two hours is that I need to pee again but I'm scared of monkeys now, maybe one will try and grab me.

Chapter 16 - Boon

December 26th

I just lie there thinking, it's all that's left. Well I could clean or tidy or write if I had anything to tidy or in all honesty any motivation. I guess that the noise made when a television isn't on any channel isn't as debilitating to others, as myself. Just a grey flickering screen with all that static, that's what this rain sounds like through a bamboo-weave wall.

I'm going to blame something from my childhood. Let's go with having to vacuum the house every week and say it brings back harrowing memories of repetitive effort and that noise, and there we have a great excuse to go back to sleep. I mean it's out of my control right?

Every six seconds a new drip hits my mosquito net - I hope the monkeys drown.

I don't really hope this, but I hope they are super soaked.

What's this? My other voice, who knows me so well, is being a pain in the neck and chimes in with, 'ummm if you know it's an excuse then it's not an excuse', or something like that. 'Hey voice! Let me sleep, it's wet and I'm lazy.' 'ummm..' By the gods not you again! '..mm you're not lazy, you've just been lying around so long you've got used to it'.

Good argument there, it seems if I were lazy the denial of this has even tricked my conscience, so I dish soaped myself up and stood outside in the rain. It had proven easier to keep my shorts on and give them a wash in the process, they might foam a bit on my way to work but these things weren't shower Clem's problem, they were walking to work Clem's problem. I looked to see what the monkeys had left on the roof, they had given my hut a little crown where they had pulled all the straw ends loose and left them standing.

Elsewhere there was another guy, a different guy. Bouncing droplets hit his shins, pooling at his feet. Boon stood just under the open second floor of the passenger ferry watching the island emerge from the fuzz of rain cutting through fog. Rain, to him, meant business.

He watched the twin peaks of the island slide past as the ship circled towards the jetty, revealing the lower features of cliffs and beaches to each side. Thai rain was just like any other rain aside from it either being non-existent or so torrential you find yourself barely standing for the weight of it. This was the latter, a tail-end of a storm at sea and it was supposed to last the rest of the night.

Any other time he would not be seen on the passenger ferry but, due to the weather, the speedboats were unwilling to make the trip across the ocean. He knew he could have easily persuaded them and avoided sharing his trip with excitable holiday makers, but he simply did not care enough. To him, everyone around would eventually become money in his pocket.

The pier road stank of sewage as drains bubbled over and sandal-clad tourists collected infections, squelching from one spot of shelter to the next. Boon knew the back roads and made his way to his first stop – the original and quieter of his two tattoo shops right near the backpacking district of the island.

'Sawadee krap,' he muttered a quick greeting as he ducked under the shutter, which had been pulled low to avoid the wind carrying rain inside. He had spent almost two weeks away from the island but for all that had changed it could have been an hour.

Boon cast his eye over the shop and was unsurprised to find it a proper mess. Cut-offs from design-transfers littered the floor around the table and unwashed dishes were piled high under the tattoo chair.

Bua was playing cards with a young westerner who couldn't have been much more than 20. Bua sprung to his feet and left the game when he saw Boon.

I stayed put, still holding a losing hand of cards, and waited. Bua sat with the newcomer like Thai people often do, bum to their heels with the soles of their feet flat on the floor, a really unique balancing act.

This must be the big boss, I thought as they leafed through those vague records Bua scribbled down after each tattoo. Each would look something like 4000/2400/1200/400 – from a 4000 baht tattoo I knew the 400 was for me, so either Bua or the boss must have got the 60% with 30% going to the other.

The southern Thai way to call someone over to join you was very different from back home - actually it was kind of the opposite. We would naturally use our 'come hither' signal to summon someone over – using one hand, with the palm facing upwards and one to four fingers raised moving together. In Thai hand-signals however, this means gesture translates to a semi-aggressive warning. The signal we would use to shoo someone away, which is basically the same as 'come here' but with our fingers and palm facing our feet and with a more abrupt waggle; well this, in Thailand, means come on over. It can also sometimes mean go away. Okay, it means several things – most important is to watch the eyes and make a judgement call.

The newcomer shooed me away from a distance, and being in Thailand I stood up, crossed the room and sat with him and Bua. He looked me in the eyes and nodded, this guy had a kind face, full of energy and future.

'Okay,' he said as he extended his hand, 'You Kim, I Boon. Big boss.'

I shook his hand and the multiple gold rings clicked together as his fingers folded around mine. He held my gaze and continued. 'You work Boon, mai?' then without a pause he affirmed, 'Kim work Boon,' nodding again.

I said, 'Okay,' because that was the theme of the week.

Boon asked, 'Kim you worry, mai?'

'Not worry,' I was thinking 'why?' but I didn't say anything.

'Not worry have Boon big boss Kim!' Boon stated as fact.

I couldn't help but notice he hadn't released my hand after the shake, so there we sat holding hands, talking about not worrying when I didn't know there were any worries.

My new boss spoke to Bua in Thai once more and left the hand-hold only when he reached across to hand the small accounts book back, and to fold a thick wodge of notes into his waistband.

So Boon left, ducking under the shutter into the rainy day, with a small wave.

'Bua?'

'Kim?'

'What do I have to worry about?'

'Now you work Boon you not have problem.'

'I didn't have any problems before.'

'So no problem.'

'Okay...'

'Okay, Kim.'

'This girl, her name is Aiko,' Lemon held a turquoise-tipped finger over a lone teenager. We were focussed right in again, watching in their time. She was standing beneath an apple tree on the edge of a steep slope that led down to this huge construction site. 'I read her diary.'

Nonplussed, I wanted to ask why, but then I remembered that this was Lemon, and 'why' didn't get me anywhere. So narrowed it to, 'Why her?'

'She's angry like me, and smart like you,' she answered with bubbles in her words, she added, 'also it wasn't very long'.

'You're angry?' I had never sensed the slightest bit of anger in Lemon. 'What's making you angry?' I asked her again in case she didn't hear the question mark at the end of the statement.

Aiko was pacing and holding a stick about half her height, broken into a point at one end. She stopped by a fallen apple, put the stick against it and pressed. Lemon avoided my last question with a curt, 'Yes, and you're smart,' before adding, 'she's been doing this every morning,' I opened my mouth but Lemon raised her hand, 'wait for it.' I waited for it.

The stick came up with the apple stuck firmly on the end. Aiko slowly brought it above her head and behind her back, turning to face the construction site's car park. 'Aaaaaand,' Lemon whispered, 'Whoosh!' The arm holding the stick flew forwards, whipping the stick after it and stopping it dead with the point facing away from the girl - while the apple flew loose. The arc of the flying fruit slammed right into the car park and exploded between two cars. She cocked her head to one side, shrugged, turned, and pushed the stick into another apple.

'She launches apples into the cars every morning before school,' Lemon says, a short chuckle through her nose, 'I was curious, so I read her diary, and now I know why.'

'What did she write?' I asked.

'She tries to make the apples hit the cars because when she does, someone gives money to her family.'

'What?!'

'Well, that's not the real reason why her family gets money, she just thinks it is,' she opened my curiosity by feeding the information in strands, 'it actually comes from her sister Akari, who sells things that she steals.' She left it wide open, but in a tone that suggested the statement was final and had explained everything.

Maybe she enjoyed my intrigue over things she knew and I didn't? 'How do you know that the money comes from ...'

'I read Akari's diary also,' Lemon winked.

'So why does she throw apples at cars?' I had to ask.

'It's fascinating really,' Lemon lit up and finally gave in on the game of taunting me, 'The first time Aiko hit a car with an apple was after a class on 'New Developments Damaging Japan' in her school, she was upset,' Lemon explained. 'The night before, Akari took a phone from a classmate and sold it to a friend, so the next morning was the first time Akari put an envelope of money through her own door for her mother to find.'

'Okay,' I followed, but blindly and lurching.

'The next week, Aiko managed to hit another car. This, just by chance, was the second time her sister left the second envelope of money for her family.'

'So Aiko thinks that when she hits cars with apples, someone sends her family money.' The conclusion was there to be seen, even if it was weak.

'Right!' Lemon gave a thumbs up, 'and now she throws apples at cars every day.'

Aiko threw herself forwards, black hair wrapped around her face as a new apple flew almost dead straight this time, skidding across the car park and losing itself under a parked truck.

'But she doesn't get money every time an apple hits a car, right?'

'Not at all, if she hits a car and money appears she will think one thing leads to the other.'

'And if ...'

'If Akari doesn't leave any money for her mother, Aiko thinks nothing of it, but if you see that she wants there to be a link, then you'll see why she ignores the times a link isn't there.' Lemon placed a cold hand on my upper arm, 'In your own words, that's just their brains.'

THUD. We both turned to see an apple bouncing off the sunroof of a Sudan, leaving a mist behind it.

'Boom!' Lemon fist pumped, 'The Masuko family will have a profitable week.'

I looked at her in astonishment. 'You're joking right?'

'Yes, I'm joking.' She furrowed her brow, looking at me like I was the weird one. 'So this made me think. What if instead of throwing apples at cars, she asked for help from someone like ...' a smirk flickered across her face, 'someone like you?'

'What?' This conversation was taking an odd turn now, 'Why would they ask me for help?'

'Because, sometimes they guess right, remember?' she quoted me again, 'And if they think someone made them, maybe they think that same someone can help them.'

'If they believed someone made them and everything around them,' I asked, knowing the answer, 'why would they think ...'

'Oh, because they want there to be a link, of course,' Lemon quoted herself this time. 'If Aiko asked that someone for help, and the next morning Akari left money for their mother, she would think that the money is that help, sent from you, and not an apple hitting a car.'

'And she will ask for help every day ...' I filled in the obvious, I knew that Lemon knew that the people asked for help, a lot. There was an unspoken accusation hanging in the air that right now I wasn't ready to deal with.

'And sometimes it will feel like it works, and sometimes ...'

'She won't think about it, because she is human.'

Chapter 17 – new year's eve

December 31st

A new year comes in the morning, alongside it a million promises of bettering oneself. 'New Year; new me' is a good one if you were looking for a lie. I guess 'new start' can be roughly translated into something like - 'fake me for a few weeks' - but we are all guilty of it.

It's a risk I just don't need to take right now and better men than me have failed, so to save myself from having to fake it for too long I have made a list of my New Year's resolutions that will start first thing in the morning.

1. ...

Chapter 18 – New Year, same same

I could see light through my eyelids, a sure sign that I hadn't made it home. Forcing them open I found my face very close to a sock. The other end of the sock was a very naked person. My vision followed my movement with a half second lag.

It looked like a nudist bus crash, bodies propped up or sprawled in every direction. I saw my T-shirt by the door, and Beth from the tattoo shop was face down on the floor. Empty bottles and cans on every surface, speakers unplugged at the wall. The bed looked like a horizontal skin market; limbs under and over each other in that special way that people sleep when they just pass out drunk.

I stepped around stripped-off clothes heaped high from the impulse of the night before. Only recognising one or two others I gathered my things and with no recollection of where I was I descended three flights of stairs and headed outside to let the sunlight direct its punishment.

My shadow sat below me letting me know it was close to midday; maybe I wasn't late for my agreed starting time 'morning'. Squinting my way down to the beach and tattoo shop, I noticed the damage from the monsoon storms had mostly been cleared away with very little visible evidence left, aside from the shift in the sand banks and deep gullies carved by water down either side of Beach road.

Bua was cooking up a storm and chilli burnt my eyes as I entered the shop.

'Hello lovely,' came out as a creepy croak

'Sawadee kaap,' he replied. Bua had been cleaning - in a sense of the word - squaring papers and piling all the dirty crockery into one corner, the bound straw brush lay in the middle of the floor, proving that it has been used for at least one sweep.

True Thai food is quite a stretch from the sticky sweet takeaway I had tried in London. Bua was playing fast and loose with the hot sauce since I finally managed to explain to him that being white doesn't mean I can't eat spicy food but it still took a few attempts to 'out spice' me before he believed it. My mouth watered as he dished out a portion of Kao Pad Krapao Chilli Basil. It tasted like heaven and burnt like hell, as it should, and was the perfect kick-start hangover cure.

A recollection from a drunken chat the night before surfaced, 'Bua?' I asked in a question starting way.

Kim?' he answered through a fried egg.

'Now I work, do I need a working permit?'

'Boon big boss, Kim.'

'Yes, yes, I know but someone told me to be careful working.'

'Now you work Boon.'

'Yes but I, I need a working visa right?'

'Kim, Kim, Kim, Boon big boss, you not worry anything, okay?'

I felt like he was avoiding the question? I asked again, 'What about immigration?'

Bua slid closer to me, 'Boon have many friend police, no problem for Kim.'

'So everything is okay?'

'Sure,' he grinned and pushed my bowl a fraction closer, caught my furrowed brow and added a final confirmation, 'yes! Kim!'

The day went slowly, At first I just assumed it was taking so much longer for the customers to surface because of the night before, but by 6pm we had only seen a few heads popping around the door and the third was Boon. 'Sawadeekrap!'

'Sawadee Boon krap'

'Kim,' Boon nodded, motioning me in the Thai way to come closer. Boon fired off Thai to Bua in an explanative sort of way, Bua nodded and Boon left the shop beckoning me after him.

We ended up at Boon's second tattoo shop, right opposite one of my favourite bars on Beach road. It had the same layout with a shutter front storage-unit turned into semi-professional hangout. There were two tattoo chairs right in the middle of the room, the walls were covered in bad quality print-outs of tattoo designs and amongst them were dog-eared photos of previous work. A customer might even believe it was art done in the shop if someone thought to remove the watermarks and web addresses from the images before printing.

An older Thai man, in his fifties perhaps, hunched over the table cleaning his fingernails into a half-eaten bowl of rice, unfolded himself as we entered the room. Boon made the introductions as concisely as possible.

'Sud, Kim, Kim, Sud.'

Sud had more ink than skin, bare feet, loose fisherman pants and a small vial of sand on a chain around his neck. 'Kim work Bua shop yes?' He asked me, extending his hand.

Boon cut in, first in Thai then in English to make sure all parties were in understanding. 'Kim you work Sud shop this night, you work Bua shop morning.' Sud nodded, I nodded, Boon nodded and left.

In time two more tattoo artists arrived; they were both young, one named Lek and the other Nu, both were covered head to toe in ink, wrapped in skinny jeans held up by fat buckles and were plastered in cheap gold bling.

My first night helping at this shop was non-stop, I could see why they needed to help. The experience of Sud, and the reassurance from me, filled the room with more people than walked past Bua's shop in a day. As we worked, we drank; each tattoo was celebrated with a shot of rice wine, and somehow I found myself taking a shot with each artist as they finished.

By 11pm Bua was called to help with the overflow of waiting customers, making four of them finishing small tattoos every hour or so; the good times were there for me. As the night bowled on they slid the music up to fist bumps and hugs. Shots, shots, shots.

Some people knew which tattoo they wanted and others just wanted something to commemorate a good feeling; who were we to judge as names went on wrists and hearts went on hips. I vaguely remember sharing a bucket of vodka-soda between two German girls as they tried to drink their way through matching infinity symbols. They took it in turns with the four-straws-super-straw I made for them so they could drink as they were inked. Smoke billowed, music blared and finally I stumbled out into the cool air.

This is when I found Boon sitting in my doorway.

'Kiiiiim! How was your night?'

I was going to ask Boon how he knew where I lived, or why he was sitting in my doorway, but instead I settled on, 'Really good! So many tattoos.'

'Good, good night Kim,' Boon picked up a push-bike from beside my house and added, 'sleep good Kim okay.'

I let myself in and face planted the mattress, where I stayed until around midday.

Chapter 19 – looking good

It may have been Monday, but these things meant nothing, just as nothing became every weekend. Weeks had passed by with nothing but good times; my aim as of now was to preserve this paradise.

I peeled myself off the sheets, held toothpaste in my mouth as I bucket washed my bits and pits then took the beach route to work. Deep tissue heat massage from above, the Thai sun set upon my back as it did the sand, baking both and making each step a little quicker than the last. When you found a plant or a post, you stopped to let the soles of your feet cool on the shaded spot. Each time it felt like it came just in time.

From where I stood for fifteen seconds in the line of a palm I could see Boon holding council with Sud, Nu and Lek. They were squatting in the dirt of a clearing not far from the new shop. I reached them to see they were crouched around a bottle of Regency Whiskey, five glasses and a bottle of coke. Aha, one of those types of meetings.

'Kim you have new clothes, mai?'

It was true, some three-quarter length light trousers from the night market. I had bought them last night for my next visa run off the island.

'Yep, you like them?' I asked, stomping my feet and letting them shake around a bit.

'Yes like, how much Thai baht?' he asked, rubbing his thumb and fore-finger together.

'Um, maybe 200 baht,' I told him, 'I need something to wear for my visa run.'

Boon looked blank. 'When you go visa?'

I told him soon, adding as an after-point, 'I'm not Thai, I need a visa to stay in Thailand.'

'Kim, how long you stay?' Boon held out his palms out flat.

An easy answer, 'I love it here, I would stay forever.'

He grinned, 'Kim work Boon now, Boon have good friend border control police.'

Interesting, I hated nothing more than the burst of the bubble leaving this place for the oil and roar of the outside world. 'You can give me a work visa?'

'Kim not need visa, Boon friend border control police,' He laughed again while the others stayed silent but chorused nodding. 'I tell you Kim, work for Boon no problem okay.' After a brief pause he said, 'Kim give trousers for Boon.'

Was it a question or ...? Boon dived into his pockets, sorting and extended two orange notes at arm's length without looking up, he was watching himself pour a whisky with his free hand. Then the coke, right to the brim and finally he raised his head, first to the money still in his hand and then to my legs. As if he was surprised I was still wearing my trousers, he brought his eyes up to mine. 'Kim?'

As I was wearing this particular pair of trousers I had a solution. Taking the two notes which had started nudging themselves towards me I asked him, 'What size? I can get you some new ones from the market.'

He looked down at his own trousers, almost sad, and then looked up excitedly like some overdone theatrical ploy. He was pulling at them with his thumb and forefinger, 'You take Boon trousers and Boon take Kim's, mai?'

'You want to swap clothes with me?' Everyone was watching me, waiting for me to accept these terms.

'Swap,' he nodded once.

'Okay ...' I didn't wear underwear, nobody did, it was too hot. With my hands down my own trousers I cupped my genitals and shook my lower half naked, stepping out of them, acutely aware of pedestrian traffic.

'Kim what you do?!' Boon went from mild incoherence of me wanting to keep my clothes on, into absolute hysterics. 'Okay, okay,' he laughed, 'Boon come back.' He scooped the trousers out of the dust and jogged into the privacy of the shop. I don't know why I didn't think of that.

I sat there, my naked butt in the dust, both hands covering myself, and waited.

'Kim?' Bua held a half whiskey coke at me. I sat there naked in the sun, whiskey in hand, the others suppressing grins as minutes passed. If I should have ever contemplated my current situation and life direction, this would have been a good time.

'Look good!' Boon exclaimed, once I had somehow snaked my way into his still sweat-damp clothes. He had to say this about me and not him because my trousers actually looked good on him and didn't need the reassurance. His on me however, looked like, well, like I was wearing trousers that were way too short. The bare ankles weren't a problem, I roll-up anyway, but the crotch region was the issue. Crammed to one side of the centre leg divide, one testicle right there with it and the other a mystery, I tried to make some space. You know when a child draws a shark attack and they always put one arm and a head sticking out of the side of the sharks grin? Yup.

'Looking good,' I lied. Whatever.

Chapter 20 – a short but strange introduction

It was dark in my little house. I was under a bed-sheet that smelled like tequila sweat; thin, synthetic and damp, and draped into shape over myself and - someone else.

A mixed commotion outside, must have been what woke me, then the door opened itself with, not a click or a squeak - but more of a breaking straw noise as it fell out of its frame. Maybe this noise is best described as a krumpf. That krumpf made way to an incredibly harsh bout of midday sun, simply letting me know I was late for work. A head sunk into the shining rectangle, black against it with a white-gold sheen around the thin mane of hair. 'Jesus! Close the door.' It wasn't Jesus.

'Hello, Kim.'

With one hand over my eyes I parted the middle fingers to peek through at Boon, just standing there. I told him 'hi', acutely aware that although I was under the sheet that I shared with my guest, this somehow made me feel more naked than actually just being naked. This feeling tripled when the second head came into view. It was small and very round.

'Hello,' it said.

The new head didn't step into the doorway, but peered into the darkness with a squint matching my squint as I peered back into the light. We squinted at one another ... seconds passed. 'S'okay?' it asked.

Boon broke the moment, stepping over the threshold of the doorframe and leading the stranger behind him. This stranger was in full police uniform, sergeant stripes and all. The illusion of nakedness heightened yet again, a medal on his breast caught the last bit of light as the door krumpfed almost closed behind him.

I wanted to be standing now - but that would have made things worse, considering the difference between feeling naked and being naked – I stayed put. In the corner of my eye-sight my first guest, the one who had actually been invited, pulled the sheet up a little, and with the tug of fabric my toes slid into view.

Boon, with a disinterested expression as if nothing strange was going on, clambered right onto the bed and sat crossed legged at the foot of the mattress.

'Mr. Kim this P-Nai,' Boon told me, then patted the bed beside himself to invite the officer in to join them. 'Kim, P-Nai him big man police.'

Nai leaned in a little, one hand forward but not open. The etiquette here of course is that you extend your hand to shake the hand that's hovering in front of you. But do you do the same when your hand has been somewhat inside someone recently? I gave a thumbs up and pulled an awkward face. P-Nai nodded once.

Boon went on, 'P-Nai very good friend me, if you have problem P-Nai help okay?' P-Nai nodded in concurrence. 'Him I tell you, him border police.'

Another nod.

'Kim,' Boon started a fresh conversation, 'Boon go away for business, Kim work Boon shop, have problem talk P-Sud.'

'How long?' I asked.

'For business,' he replied, and added, 'Kim look the money when Boon not here, Boon trust.'

'Not a problem,' but it didn't' make sense why I would be the one to hold onto all the profits.

'P-Nai will come in one week, to Boon shop,' Boon explained, 'him take money from Kim, okay?'

'Okay ...'

Obviously there was nothing more on the agenda and, just as impromptu as it started, the first in-bed meeting between the boss, the policeman, the lost boy and the naked girl came to an end.

Chapter 21 – touché Thailand

'Kim,' Lek waved me forth the moment he saw me come in, he sat on the stool his feet folded beneath him, using an old stand-alone computer that we copied people's photos onto, for printing tattoos that we hadn't even been involved in the design or application of. 'Have Facebook, mai?'

The familiar blue banner bar of the world's most popular social media website was already on the screen, asking us to *Sign up, it's free and always will be.*

'Have,' I nodded.

'Lek want,' he slid the keyboards around to face me. Bua and Nu had now joined the party, both at his side smiling at me. Bua was wearing a gold headband and, for the first time ever, a top - he had chosen an open brown shirt that he tucked in all around, right to the front.

'Sure,' I joined them. I wasn't sure, something about social media invaded the atmosphere of the island but I couldn't say 'yes' for myself and then not open an account for them. 'Okay,' I settled in, 'what's your email address?'

'No email,' Lek shook his hands at the screen, 'Facebook.'

'I see,' I knew where this was going, and quickly set up an email account, fighting the protest but not taking the time to explain further than 'you need email for facebook'. 'Do you want your name in English or name in Thai?' I mimicked writing with my right hand, blank faces. 'English name okay?'

'Okay,' Lek repeated, 'for English girl.' Now I knew why we were doing this. I typed *Lek* into the name bar.

'Bua,' said Bua.

'Yes, Nu,' said Nu.

They were both pointing to the name bar, 'This is Lek's account,' I told them, 'I can make you one.'

'No, account,' Lek gestured a finger circling the three of them, 'all account us.'

'That's not how it ...' I changed my story, 'Okay, what's your names, Lek Bua Nu, second name Tattoo?'

Bua had the answer, seemingly a totally random word, 'Yak Sapairo!' he said with pride.

'Yak Sa-pairo?' I tried to repeat the strangely pronounced word, deleting *Lek* and hovering over the 'Y'

'Bua name Yak Sapairo,' he stabbed his untipped bamboo rod at his own chest, 'you know?'
I did not know, this word was a new name - but it could be their collective facebook name, sure, I pressed '*Y...A...K*'

'No! Kim, Yak, Ya,' Bua waved my hands off the keyboard, holding backspace down for the three letters, 'Ya' he scanned the keyboard and pressed the '*J*' repeating 'Yak Sapairo' and posing, his head high and proud.

What was I even looking at here?
Lek and Nu managed absolute union both gesturing to Bua with their hands, 'JAK SAPARO!'

By the gods - Jack Sparrow! 'Oh Jack Sparrow!' I said out loud.

'Yes, Kim, Yak Sapairo.' Bua nodded enthusiastically, so I set up the triple owner social media account under the name Jack Sparrow, uploading a photo of the three of them standing around the tattoo chair holding their bamboo kits at off angles. That was that.

The Facebook page was a bad idea, I knew it already, trying to explain which artist would be doing someone's tattoo while all three of them clustered around the monitor giggling and pointing. Each and every time I looked over there was a different girl on the screen, they were hitting keys furiously but I didn't know how much they could type in English. The outcome, whatever it was, would be nothing but funny.

Sud was curious about the whole thing but didn't want to be part of the online stalking perversion. Although he did ask a lot of questions.

'This one, you just write small things that you want to share.' He was asking about Twitter.

'Share for who?'

'To anyone, your friends or people who follow you.'

'Share music, mai?'

'Not this one, only words – anything under 140 characters.'

'Characters?'

'140 characters so maybe eighteen words or something.'

'Share eighteen words to people here?'

'Yes, that's about it.'

'Why people do this Kim?'

I was stumped, totally. 'I ... because, they want to,' was my best response. Touché Thailand, touché!

It took the Facebook trio less than an hour to get kicked off the platform. When I typed www.fa' into the search bar, a multitude of recently visited profile links dropped down. I had one assumption - that they had been sitting there systematically '*friending*' girls they didn't know, using the profile Jack Sparrow - Status: Single, Interested in: Women, Works at: Tattoo' and sporting their three grinning faces, topless, 90% tattooed and adorned in cheap gold.

It wasn't a surprise that they had been reported, but they didn't ask for another account. That was it, the online adventure, for them, was over.

I made a mental note to log-out every time I used the computer.

January 29th
The ten centimetre murk of half decomposed leaves turned a little as I disturbed the surface of the 90 litre dustbin that acted as my shower and flush, it was only a little cooler than my hand as I scooped one of the last jugs of fresh water I needed to rinse the soap off. The wash-off splashed around my feet instantly shrinking in the midday sun, I threw my scooping tub back into the water and watched it sink as I towelled off. No sign of that lizard for a while, maybe I had avoided certain repercussions that came from messing with nature.

A penetrating wail bounced from wall to wall, it was an alarm, a moaning screech projecting from the hotel-top loudspeakers around the island. I had a few guesses flitter through my mind, but there was one that had sat in the back since I had heard stories of entire Thai islands being wiped out in a matter of hours – Tsunami!

I flew out of my bathroom with my shorts barely up, smashed my door back on itself and turned to see, well to see, what everyone else was doing I suppose. They were running!

I knew the system, it was on all the signs around the jungle edges 'Tsunami Evacuation Zone' in block capitals accompanied an arrow that pointed towards the nearest path up the foot of the mountain. People had dropped their bags, left their shops open, stopped mid-tattoo and run – I flew behind them, toes burning on the road, dodging the crowd clamouring up the 'V' funnel into the trees I took a jump over the bank of the stream that cut past my house, knowing that beyond the first layer of undergrowth was a clear run to the hilltop.

There we sat, listening to Dane; 'the system in place is like a sensor that can feel an irregular movement in the ocean and ...' Dane told me about the alarm, his voice a drab tone like an idling engine. It had been twenty minutes sitting and the wail went on, warning people to join us on the high ground. I could see the sea from my perch, sitting alongside so many others huddled amongst trees, flies and mosquitoes. '... is unlikely as before a tidal wave like the last one, the sea is sucked away from the beach, and as you can see the tide down there is still in soooo I think it's just a false alarm,' he paused and then added, 'so that's good.'

It was good, but false alarm or not I decided to stay away from the death zone for a little longer and, as Dane was somehow making tidal waves seem dull, I took a stroll through 'camp beachwear-in-the-jungle' – a strange sight on mass. I headed a little higher to get some air, and then a little higher still until I found myself jogging up a path I had never found before - then running. Just over the next leafy crest and turning an impromptu left I sensed a change in light hinting at a clearing, hands together in front of me to part the hanging vines I almost ran clean off a jut of rock that was sticking out of the side of the jungle.

Before I stumbled to a stop I didn't know I was even close to the cliff, it must have been the one flat face you could see from the beach but could never find on a hike, and atop of it must be this platform. Grey rock, hot and soft, I took a few more steps out onto the ridge, the green overhang around the opening barely let it protrude past the cave of hanging bushes and tangled vines, even two steps from the edge leaves fluttered in my peripheral vision. My heart still pounding I sat, and I felt solace amongst madness.

February 5th

'Hi guys, I notice you're addicts. What is it you're addicted to?' no that won't work very well, um, 'Oh, hi, didn't see you there, why, what is that in that little foil cone?' yes this sounded a little less judgemental. I was wording a question that through the previous five days had made itself into one; it turns out that twenty-hour days non-stop tattooing isn't fuelled by passion, but by a pretty serious drug addiction. I felt it would be a bit abrupt to say, 'Hello, what's wrong with your face, is that a narcotic soaking into your brain?' so my morning went like this:

'Hi Noi, hi Dow.' Noi looked up and down again, Dow smiled. I hadn't seen them in a short while, the shop had been monopolising my time and Boon was talking about more projects in the future. 'So Dow, can you tell me something?'

'What is it?'

'The guys I work with in the tattoo shop?'

She furrowed her brow, I could tell before that she didn't like the scene at all, 'Yes ...?'

'Do they take a lot of drugs do you think?'

'Meth.'

'What?'

'Thai language we call it yaba, English call it meth,' she said offhand. 'They smoke a lot?'

'They smoke something every day.'

'Not a lot, this is normal,' she swallowed, 'for tattoo boy.'

'Okay, meth, hey, well that's definitely a bad idea.' This gave me some clarity as to why I was the one trusted in holding hundreds of thousands of Baht for Boon, and not the others.

'Yes, bad idea but yaba good for work,' she told me, 'cheap drug Thailand, many people take.'

'I knew it was something, meth is pretty serious huh?'

'Very yes, in Thai language yaba mean 'crazy medicine' because it make people lose their head one day.'

Later on I got to a google search. It wasn't great news and didn't help my security doubts. More than half of the world's meth was being taken in South-East Asia and the results were a bit grim. It seemed that this was the drug propping up the south-east Asia red light district and funding the Thai mafia. An image search or what to look out for confirmed to me that, yes, my artists were indeed smoking meth, all day. Well now!

I could easily guess that the police weren't particularly concerned about this. P-Nai had been to the shop twice now, the first time to collect all of the profits, and the second time to return the same money, well not the same money but the same amount, and then to collect what we had made up until then. Explaining off-hand that the money he was leaving was for me to give as change to the tourists and that the money used to pay for tattoos was better kept to one side for Boon when he returned. It was hard to ignore the truth and you didn't need to know a lot about drugs and organised crime to work out that I had been inadvertently laundering money through a shop that ran on meth fumes.

I couldn't help but feel like this was a bad idea in the long run.

Chapter 22 – three men and the devil

For these three men, I'll break the rules I made myself and take you back stage in their lives, pulling their past into this story, at least how they had told it to me.

I bring you Sud, honest Sud. Diving for cockles under the pier before school, a good boy, from a poor family – even worse off than most. Sud lost his way long before his classmates, and saw the darkness of the inside of a cell before he turned eighteen. It was in that darkness, before his eyes had time to adjust, that he met her. First name 'Ya' last name 'Ba.' She was the one who taught him how to run from his problems without looking back. She loved power and the tricks she could play - urging him to sell his soul for her and steal for her until she knew he would always find his way back to her.

It was not love at first sight, but after the first night and his first time, he thought of nothing else. Her friends took him under their wings and told him just what she wanted from him– they taught him how to live for her, just like they did. Inspired by her, he learned a fast trade - no food, no sleep - tapping into the darkness he became an artist. His single season passed in Bangkok central jail and she stuck to her promise - she didn't leave him. She followed him out the wrought gate into the world he once knew, the same sea, the same sky – the same except for that one extra cloud, perpetually following him south, never far behind.

Into the spotlight, big screen sun-beam smile - Nu was always an island boy. He had avoided bad company by working hard, an outlet for his expressive side he put ink into skin with impeccable precision. The money he made he saved and sent home to his mother, sister and baby brother, so they could have a better life. Nu met Sud as a mentor, not a bad man I must implore, but 'Ya' was there she wanted more – when her followers are weak she will speak for them. She asked Nu to join her, just once, in the bungalow behind the bar - it wouldn't take long. He did, as people do, follow his mentor's advice. From then his tune became a skipping track, the needle jumping a splitting crack. As it goes, always, without fail - Nu needed more of that scent, her impulse, the energy and her confidence. He asked Sud how this could happen, it was easy he said, cut out the middle man. Talk to Boon, take the meth not the money, this way he would never lose his sweet Ya Ba.

The third man, named himself Lek. The lover, the killer. The perfectionist of a swagger, the charismatic aura. Born on a high tide and a black moon Lek was destined to meet her too, it came before Sud, and long before Nu. She made him angry and horny and sad and frustrated. He did things he never would have fathomed without her. She made him brave to move fast and not think, and when the judge banged the gavel down he didn't blame her at all.

She was loyal of course, joining him deep in the darkness of the cells, camping out behind loose tiles between two bars. Available when he needed her kiss. When he left she came with him, her grip was true on charismatic Lek. Now the mainland of Thailand was different to the islands, people could see her standing by his side and with his history of convicted violence her hold on him was hard to hide. He crossed the ocean to a land with no law, hoisted her flag and like that he was accepted by her people. That island of paradise and hidden addiction was a refuge for their kind, keep it hidden the best you can from the tourists and you'll survive.

I sat with the three men. My own need for escape made me the runner. Running away from monotony and normality - I had found a place far enough from what I called 'the grey fuzz.' Unknown to myself, a new mist had descended, a mix of satisfaction, denial and delusion. I call it the island eyes.

I had seen her with them, and smelt her. She sweated chemicals from their pores, pulled them into full focus and kept them up all through the night. I wasn't curious about her, not for myself. I had heard enough stories to know Ya didn't take prisoners. I had heard tell of how she eroded that line between right and wrong and kissed your fists before you struck a friend. I didn't trust her, but I wasn't scared of her. Not yet.

So a scene is set; the four men like no others, all bare chests and three gold chains. Citrus mist plumed from the Bua's nails as he dug deep into a fresh orange. It gathered the orange streetlight and settled. I was so into it, the entire array. Hedonism as I knew it then. By now the answer was always yes, but today wasn't a good time to be unaware. It was in the air, the familiar feeling of unwary and poised tension. 'Hello, Ya.'

The ridge of my thumb had become rough and thick from pushing the lid off the top of each bottle. Three shot glasses slid to join my own. Lek was hunched, repeating fine lines on an intricate design – I zoomed in on the precision of a moving pencil with fragments of graphite popping as he pressed. This concentration wasn't human but I knew that because I could feel her in here, standing over him.

The bottle tipped and filled four. Chink, clink, drink - bad ideas laid the foundations as Bua took the bottle to pour four more and four more. Fumes burnt our eyes, rising from a concoction that was fit to clean wounds or strip paint, best taken in one. I had become aware that alcohol shortened her fuse and put them on edge. Still in that soft light with the bubbles rising from the neck to the base of an upturned bottle, I watched the shot brim, knowing full well that I was dripping blood in the shark infested waters – I let the island eyes ignore it, so that I didn't have to.

Freeze frame. Pan to the man outside the door, a drunk mounting a bike - my bike to be exact. Click - the chain engaged and that was his mistake. Ya had lain dormant thus far tonight but, as always, had been waiting for an excuse just like this. I opened my mouth to curb the situation, let the man know he was in plain sight. Three heads turned like wolves and Ya took the stage - triggered by a fine hair out of place she revelled in a kneejerk reaction. The fool on the bike pushed a pedal down and became a fool in motion. She cracked her whip and the three men she knew so well left their chairs, shouting out, bare feet making for easy acceleration, leaving me sitting – the fool on the bike made for an exit stage right, still unaware.

I changed perspective kicking the table aside and made it onto the street just as the others reached the man on the bike – this is when he became aware. Thrown clear back from the vehicle, smack with a tight fist in the neck. Crack, his head hit the planet. The scene - cinematic, the bike with one wheel spinning flat one cocked to the road. The fool screamed out!

This was already enough, too much, I knew it. But Ya doesn't know how to stop, she loves to take it too far. The man rose into a kick to the spine - soft hands meeting the metalwork - his face stopping the wheel mid-spin. I was in time to catch one closed fist- but not another, losing it into the fool's teeth. '*Move!*' I mouthed to the man on the ground as he fell back again, ruby red spilling from a contorted mouth, eyes welling shut.

'Move or you will die,' spilled from my mouth. The man kicked out like a zebra with teeth in its hind, a desperate wail with his hands to his jaw. I put two arms outstretched to hold back these friends of mine, giving the scrabbling man a gift of two seconds. I was shouting through Ya to reach the men underneath, trying to be heard through her sick song, 'Enough! Enough!' until metres grew between them and their target.

Ya howled at the moon with her pack mentality, the sound reached Lek, who raised an empty bottle. I stepped forward, as if to upright my bike, but temporarily caused Lek to lose sight of the man as he disappeared into the night.

'Somewhere around here,' I slid a stack of notes, sketches and ideas to one side, more than likely burying them only deeper.

'It's a photograph?'

'They are photographs,' I told her, 'somewhere in this mess.'

I palmed some childhood pictures under a drawing board before Lemon could catch sight of them and kept reluctantly rooting through my desktop-pile filing system. She had asked me to tell her how my world looked, you know, before the borders. I really wish I had just explained it, but no, I told her that I could show her. Now I regret this, an enticement that simply led to her wanting to see them, she didn't agree to wait for the next morning. 'You live right there!' she said, and then, 'So are you going to invite me?' but a good excuse didn't come up fast enough. So here we are.

The white back of a picture parted itself from the chemical constructs I had been working on, introducing new things one by one so as not to upset the balance of things. Each time I tried a new chemical or element the people found all sorts of uses for it, but putting compounds together took time and now I shared that with the girl to my left. 'This might be it …' I flipped the picture, it was the first I had ever taken, and strange to see now.

'Oh, wow!' Lemon spoke as she did when she first saw my globe, with that same soft awe.

I found another a few shuffles later, 'Here you go.' I held it to her and she took it but her eyes didn't leave the first.

She spoke slowly and in shallow breaths, 'What have they done to your world?'

'Who?' I asked, knowing what she meant.

'The humans, they changed the colour of the planet.'

'Slightly,' I said, and then I admitted, 'to an extent.'

'You have to tell me,' Lemon fixed her eyes to mine; it was uncomfortable.

'What?'

'You didn't know this would happen?'

'I mean ...' I started to explain.

The argument stayed with us all the way back to the hidden place by the pond.

'But when you first decided to put people here, you didn't know what they would be like?' A new light had entered her eyes; is this the anger she alluded to?

'Lemon, listen ... Look!' I tried to rationalise with her. I lifted the sheet and went to turn the globe but remembering how she felt about that just circled my hand over it like some sort of mystic. 'Ahem,' I knew there were good people, not that she was in the mood to hear it, yet I reminded her, 'There are a lot of good people too.'

'Like who?' she asked. She knew there were good people. Lemon was normally more receptive and forgiving, in the way that if I was struggling to explain something, she would fill in the blanks. Not today.

'Okay yes, the dark is hard to ignore,' I agreed, 'but before this orb there was air, and now look ...' I zoomed in on the island again, I knew the time of day and exactly where to look.

'What's that?' Her natural curiosity softened her intended abruptness.

'She feeds stray cats,' I told her. The beautiful girl from Sweden often sat at a desk facing the street, the desk part was her job but she spent more of her time on the floor, nursing an armful of kittens.

'They are her cats, she has to feed them.' Lemon challenged my point. What happened to the days when she pointed out the beauty and I needed persuading? This is what happens when you pay attention too long.

'They are sick cats from the street, I saw a boy bring her two more this week – one was so infected its eyes were sealed shut.'

'Which one?'

'That one,' I pointed out the runt, a feeble grey and white with a cocked tail.

'Its eyes are fine,' Lemon's tone accusing me of stories.

'They are now!' I looked her in the eyes this time, hoping I could hold it. 'She wipes them, feeds them and cleans them all day long.'

'Okay, that is pretty incredible, but this is still her work.'

'No, her work is sending tourists on boat trips,' I set my point into action, 'she does this because she is a good person.'

'One good person!' Lemon was being a bit of an ass right now, if she wasn't so perfect I would have told her so, but instead I asked her what difference it made, she had a double barrel reply-gun ready and pointed at my chest. 'The tiger temple.'

She had been there before, I knew it because she slid her eyes right to the enclosure.

'Do animals pray to you?' she asked, voice calm and dark but without waiting for a reply she said, 'If they do, there would be a lot of pleas for help coming from in there.'

Guilt. It hurt my chest. I had seen it before, and passed it over as human evolution of compassion. I just did not want to delve too deep. 'The tigers ...'

'Please don't defend them,' I could feel the angst and anger coming off her body in waves. 'Not now.'

Emotions were not my forte; I glanced sideways and immediately back, the tears in her eyes were the last thing I wanted.

Then she said what I had been hoping not to hear, because it was a thought that passed through my mind almost every day, 'What are you going to do about it?'

Chapter 23– Soul Sister

The curls below the peacock's fantail nearly touched its back leg, which was cocked back in a strut, the shading would have to be light and impeccable. This wasn't a problem; every man here, save for me, was an expert with the needle and Sud was always fair when he chose who would take the job on. He and I were the ones who had copied and edited several of her favourite pieces together, tracing and transferring them onto the skin.

Josafine lay on her side, centre shop, a sarong covering her breasts and another folded under her to keep her hips high and straight. She had the air of a girl who would normally be a lot of fun, but under the weight of the decision, a side tattoo the size of a dinner plate was keeping her sober. As the transfer wrapped around Sud smoothed the creases to fit with her body shape and peeled the last of it off.

She sat up slowly keeping her entire upper body straight so she wouldn't smudge the ink, popping herself off the chair and facing the mirror.

'Oh my god I love it!' her reflection put its hand to her mouth, the other still holding the sarong in place. 'I love it, I love it, I love it, okay! How much?'

A screech and a slam came from behind, I spun to see Lek reaching up and wrenching the second shutter down, stopping it around two feet from the shop floor. Angry shouting in Thai came spraying out of his mouth, at this speed undecipherable to me.

He looked different, wired, manic and maybe a little excited. Both knees hit the floor and he folded sideways until his shoulder was level with them, watching the space under the shutter, the feeling of the room had sunk like a stone. When nobody moved, neither did I. Click. It went black.

Eyes adjusting to the lights being shut off I made out Lek reaching under to the armchair that occupied the space between the doors. He rustled for a moment and then pushed up with his wrist, leaning the seat back against the wall. Something caught the light and from under the chair, my chair, and out came a shiny but dated revolving chamber handgun.

I turned to Sud, 'What the fuck?!' Then I saw the unsheathed knife Sud was passing from hand to hand. In the half-light Lek was raising the gun, stopping its path as it was pointing right at my face. Those two seconds held on a little too long before 'click'. He had popped the chamber to one side, effectively disarming the gun but, purposefully, to show me the blocked bullet holes - proof that it was loaded. What sort of theatrical parade was this?

I moved a millimetre before the gun jerked up, momentum closing the chamber as it stopped parallel to his jaw, the elbow resting on his knee. I tried to hold back on any reaction until I knew who was going to get shot. The tension gripped the base of my throat, and out of the corner of my eyes Josafine slid to her knees. Nu could have been a mannequin for all the moving he was doing.

The gun owned the room. Click. Sud let his rings touch the blade as it rolled in his fingers. They waited, for something. I tried to control my breathing. Click. Click.

I didn't notice any music until a new song came on; the heightened awareness of danger had blocked that out. Now it was impossible to ignore, crisp and clear singing through the door, the vocals of Soul Sister by Train cut into the air, I watched the tip of the barrel hovering just above the opening, transfixed.

The song sliced into the darkness... A shadow passed close by the opening. In my peripheral vision the knife that turned in Sud's fingers stopped dead. It should be almost impossible to bear but the clearly versed lyrics played on, mocking the moment. Nu repositioned his feet slightly.

Bang! Something hard fell flat by my feet - a feeling as if someone had pushed my heart right up into my throat. Josafine, who I had truly forgotten was there, had knocked the table on its side in a desperate move towards the gap below the shutter. She put both hands in the light from the opening, pulled herself forwards slapping the floor with her front and then, holding out one palm in the direction of the loaded gun, she scrabbled through the gap and lurched out of sight.

'That was smart,' I thought to myself, 'she was in here with these maniacs, and now she's not ... I should do that.' Any sudden movement however, to me, seemed like a dangerous one ever since I had gotten to know the unpredictability of Ya – so I took one step. Sud stared out of the darkness and shook his head, the strip of light reflecting from the floor made his face look like it had been carved in an old tree.

Clean and punctuating, each line of the song taunted the situation... I took another step, breathing slow. This mix of moment and music was the epitome of contrapuntal by now, eventually something had to give and as close to a minute passed with no movement inside or outside of the shop.

Lek spoke first, 'Kim go, take girl.'
I didn't point out that Josafine was long gone. Hesitant to move too fast, I sidestepped towards the door.

He spoke again 'Kim, have big problem, not okay. Go!' So as Train rang out the final note I took a deep breath, slid out into the streetlight and stood up.

The general throb of tourists mulling around the bar hadn't changed one bit; the massage shop at the end of the road still had its usual shady queue. There was actually nothing going on at all. I thought about telling them that all was status quo in the outside world, so they could stop crouching in the dark staring at the floor, but I had taken enough of their meth-addled crap for a week, so I just walked away.

The crab – episode 3

The crab watched the island appear and vanish, wave after wave. The wind blew in erratic gusts caused by a change in air pressure. The sky deepened and layered thick above the sinking sun as it dipped between the mountains and illuminated the underside of the forming cloud bank; a striking scene.

As the land cooled the rain began to fall, thick and fast from the first drop, pulling a soft glow from the last slice of sunset. From blood-orange to black in minutes, the brewing storm stood on a hundred-thousand liquid legs and stamped at the land below. The crab stared at the island's silhouette, crouched on the horizon under the merciless tirade of a true monsoon.

Zoom into the scene ahead, between the falling raindrops and away from the floating flip-flop.

Chapter 24 – heavy rain

Breach the beach and follow a powerful front of air pushed by the storm. The wind pushed the rain horizontal as it stripped palms, barraged homes and hit the side of a straw roof, catching the underside and half tearing the rough steel ridge from its fastenings.

Seven feet below I was hit in the face by a lot of water. I opened my eyes to a split second of moonlight that vanished with an unnerving clap - what the hell was that? I sat up trying to locate myself; the space around the shuddering door gave unnerving pulses of blue light but told me I was in bed. So why am I wet?

I wiped the hair away from my eyes as the entire world relocated an inch to the left. Moonlight and thunder from above made me squint into another bout of lukewarm water as it hit me in the face. This was new and, most likely, bad news.

Another hard stare into the darkness should clarify the situati ... Whump! The whole hut shifted backwards dumping more swampy water. With each splash, moonlight entered the room and with a clash the whole bamboo box returned to near black. I knelt and ran my hand up the wall by the foot of the bed, finally finding the light switch. Click, click, no luck ... but this was probably a good thing, considering it's raining inside.

The wind roared around the outside the hut and delivered punches to the flimsy walls; I watched as the roof dropped a small dirty swimming pool onto the mattress. With one almighty howl the whole room lit up, and as the storm cracked its electrical whip, turning the skies white, I could see the folded metal sheet above me standing tall on end, before turning and slamming back down into place along with the darkness it commanded. I kicked the door clean out of the frame.

The dirt road was now a mud bed lying under inches of water that danced around my ankles. I turned to look at the hut, standing alone in the moonlight, bowing and begging for relief. It was late and my mental state had already started to deteriorate, autopilot took over. I dug my fingers in through the underside of the thatch and wrapped them over the upper edge of the wall supports, sharp but bearable. I hooked one foot on a broken stump and with some effort managed to elbow and knee my way up onto the thatch slope, making sure to keep my limbs wide so it didn't all cave in, taking me with it.

Some mercy was doled out as the wind dropped momentarily to give me the chance to reach high onto the metal ridge to ease myself towards the top. Mercy gave way to mockery as the gale took a turn, hitting the sheet with enough force to snatch it from under my palm, letting my face slap flat into the thatch.

Automatically my fingers dug into the straw again, so I didn't slide off completely, to be snatched back as I glanced up to see the tyrannical metal blade coming down towards them. I dug the inside of one leg deep into the roof to stop myself falling back, feeling nail heads under the straw push through the skin. It had to be ignored, levering off anywhere I could feel a bamboo beam under my knee, I caught the same hand on the edge of the fold and bore down with my fingertips.

Remember this moment? This is the moment when you first joined me, lying flat on that roof, drowning in thin air, about to lose my grip once more.

I sat on that little house, on the roof that didn't work if I wasn't on top of it to hold it down. Just two feet below me, a light bulb that leaked, dripping onto a bed you could swim in, surrounded by four walls still being barraged from the inside and out because of that special kind of door that just *wasn't*.

The overriding pain was from my upper chest, like my nipple was cut in half or close to it, but this seemed almost worth it as the view from up here was a spectacular, manic, panoramic of chaos.

'Kim what you do, mai?' I peered below to see Dow's father with one hand held over his brow as he tried to turn his face to me without being pummelled by rain.

'I am on the roof ... and I can't move!'

He just stood there. The path was a stream now, parting around his bare feet. His forehead crinkled into a question.

'Oh, right ... because the metal bit here is coming off and I am sitting on it,' I explained. It made perfect sense to me to act as a pseudo-roof until the storm calmed itself.

He took a few seconds and muttered and shook his head, then turned and sploshed back to his hut. I just sat there. Was it possible that the roof was slowly sinking under me? Maybe I'm a few cracked beams away from being back in bed, presumably with a few cracked ribs to join them.

Dow's father returned with a large roll of pink plastic twine. 'Can use this mai?' he said, mimicking throwing the ball to me.

And so we commenced playing a game that I would like to call 'old man throwing things just out of reach.' The twine ball sailed right past me and into the dirt on the other side of the hut. I looked down; he shook his head as he waded around the front of the house to try again. This happened for a while, it sailed much faster from left to right, than it did against the wind in the opposite direction. One time it landed on the slope above my foot, splat into the straw and as I shifted to try to hook it up with my toe the ball started unravelling itself down the thatch and back into the mud.

The next throw was with the wind, featuring an almost completely unravelled tangle of twine; it was less of a 'catch' and more 'me being netted like a fish.' I untangled myself and let the loose end drift back to him on the wind, shouting, 'Tie that to something!' trying to make myself heard through turmoil. My ancient accomplice caught onto the plan and soon the cord was tight. 'Now the other side!' I called down, gathering up most of the twine but throwing a long loose loop down that side - sure enough something pulled it tight. As each length was pulled and tied I felt the metal sheet pull away from my body and closer into the roof, until finally it was tight enough to warrant my dismount.

After falling flat in the dirt, when my numb-weakened legs hit the slush and didn't work for the first few seconds, we collected ourselves and carried on throwing the re-rolled ball to each other over the hut, tying it off each time and moving our position up and down until the whole house looked like it had been caught in a lazy spider's pink web.

There was laughing and shaking of heads, but I was feeling pretty finished. I tried to get clean by wiping my hands over my face trying to clear the filth and by scooping the water from the small street-side stream to wash it down my legs. The underside of my forearms stung fiercely where the dirt had been ground into all the cuts and scratches, I was aware of the taste of my hair running over my lips, metallic and salty all at once. My fingers throbbed and prickled as the blood returned to the tips.

The hut was dark again but I didn't need the moonlight to know that I couldn't sleep here tonight, the steady drip hitting the mud puddle down the centre of my bed, falling through exposed electrical wiring, convinced me to go to the tattoo shop where, hopefully, I would find some calm, safety and sanity.

It was still raining pretty hard so I pulled it up and back down right behind me, surprised to step into a fully lit shop. All three of them were there; Lek and Nu were folded motionless into one of the two tattoo chairs like puppies in an undersized cage - I realised this might have been the first time I had ever seen them sleeping.

Sud was on the other end of the spectrum, it took me a few seconds to decipher what I was looking at. He crouched in the corner of the room, both hands above his head gripping hefty chunks of hair in his left, and with the other, which was wrapped at an odd angle around a pair of scissors, he was hacking through the tufts and letting them pile up between his feet.

'Sud?' I stared at the man, hunched so much that his Buddha medallion sat between his feet and his knees touched his armpits. I knew that stench. The smell of Ya filled the room. I picture her, tall behind the man, thin strings from her fingers, tight with control. She tweaked a thumb and his head jerked up.

Sud, eyes like the moon, looked right through me, he said, 'Sud.'

Her claws were dug deep, I told him, 'Yes that's you, you're Sud.'

The faint clicking of his thick hair parting between the closing blades paused for a moment. 'Sud,' he muttered into the distance.

'Sud ... what are you doing?'

He said nothing at first, not even his name again, then as if it caused him physical pain to do so, his eyes slid into focus and onto me. Slowly he pushed through into my dimension and joined me in the same room. 'Kim!' he exclaimed in delight.

'Hey Sud, whatcha doing?'

Sud told the truth, 'Sud take off Sud hair. Uh-huh.'

'Okay, okay, that's true'

'Nee a-rai?' Nu, had been woken by the conversation and leaned over the back of his chair, 'Kim what happen?'

I followed his eye-line to where I was standing. There was a small puddle around my feet and in the light I could see that most of the mud and bits of straw had evaded my quick wash down. 'I was fixing my roof and ...'

'Kim crazy.'

'Me? Me crazy? Look at Sud, what is Sud doing with his hair?' Right on cue, a new fistful touched down between his bare feet.

'Sud him take off him hair.'

'So he is the crazy one.'

'Kim, you swim, mai?' Nu laughed.

It was such a surreal moment, 'Nu, how about we ignore all this' I motioned to my lower half, 'and pay attention to that.' I waved in the direction of Sud, who somehow, completely silently, was now standing.

He was looking at me as if he had just seen me for the first time in weeks, 'Kim?!'

'Sud are you okay?'

'Sud take off Sud hair.'

'Can I ask why?'

'Sud shoot gun.'

'What?!' Maybe I didn't want to know the answer to my next question, 'At someone?'

'Sud go to see Judge.'

'What, now?'

'Morning,' he exhaled slowly and with a shake.

I asked, 'You have to see the judge, for what?' I moved over to join him. His every breath smelled like warm metal.

Eyes dilated I watched him go back inside his head in search for an answer and when he returned, 'Sud shoot gun.'

I put two and two together. Shaving your head to meet a superior was a sign of respect and very much expected before a court appearance, so this could explain the hair. I turned to ask a less drug addled Nu but he had gone back to sleep. Instead I asked Sud in one last attempt for a coherent answer 'Tell me you didn't shoot anyone? ... maybe if you did, just say you didn't, that would be good'

'Sud shot up,' he spoke slowly shakily raising two fingers to the roof, 'ghost'.

Ghost? You know, I didn't need to know what that meant, but what could I do? I took the scissors from him and placed them well out of reach and taking a clean razor from the cabinet I helped him into the tattoo chair and slowly started shaving his head. It took a while, tapping out thick varying lengths of hair with each scrape. The few digs and scratches he had already made were shallow and not too visible from the front, so with some time and attention I had a good chance of making him look presentable for his court appearance.

He was sleeping where he sat by the time I had finished, I wiped his dome over with a shirt I found under the sofa and lay him down. I decided to stay with him until the morning where I would wake him just after sunrise in time to take the first boat off the island and into town, but after a few hours of trying to sleep with the chemical smell of meth-sweat filling my nostrils, combined with my unwashed skin itching all over, I gave up and slid out. It was still a while before sunrise so I took some tools and went to my hut to salvage what I could.

When the sun split the clouds the morning light hit my little house, it was looking more than sorry for itself, somehow worse than I had remembered in the chaos of the night before. I dug out what I could, loose change and a very muddy toothbrush, things like that. Propping the mattress against a tree to dry in the Thai sun, I hung the sheets and clothes from the branches around it, but before I turned to the task of fixing the house itself I would need to fix myself, and then send Sud on his way.

First stop was the pharmacy. I'm risking your judgement here; little or no sleep had become normality and easy to fix with what we all called 'diet pills.' They were over-the-counter tablets you could buy for 50baht, but in truth are nothing different to what we in the Western world call 'speed.' It was an easy fix for a few nights of no rest, even if it did make you stare at things a little too long. They would take twenty minutes to kick in so I washed two down on my way to the shop to check on Sud, timing was everything.

I arrived to open shutters and a newly shaved Sud sitting on the sofa spooning noodle soup into his mouth. 'Ready, mai?' I asked him, expecting a yes or a no. Sud looked at me completely blank. 'Ready to see judge, mai?' I ventured once more.

'See judge?' I wasn't surprised really, nothing came completely unexpected anymore. It had been a 24hour tirade of unexpected trials and tribulations but it turned out that the biggest surprise of the day belonged to Sud; when he woke with a clean-shaven head.

'Kim!' a memory passed behind his tired eyes 'Why you cut off Sud hair?' His face and tone demanded an answer.

It was funny - but also a little worrying. My brain wanted to say, 'You know what? I give up,' the warning signs of a vice taking over a mind are hard to ignore but was I ready to turn my back on everything yet? I took the deepest breath and concentrated harder than ever on my rose tinted world. 'This isn't that bad,' I told myself.

'About it?' I defended my position and doubted it at the same time. 'You know I can't do anything!'

'You can!' she snapped, 'but you won't!'

'*You* were the one who said not to change anything!'

She curled her hands, facing inwards, as if shaking an invisible ball of frustration. 'I said not to *hurt* them, there is a big difference.'

You see, Lemon came into my life with pre-installed compassion. It seemed to be her upbringing, nurture, and experiences that shaped her heart. Due to her nature, I am sure, the love for all that is good came easily, but from all that I can see, this love was learned. We had spent too long on one spot, watching the people in one corner of my complex globe and it was not going well.

The tiger temple was run, incredibly, by the Buddhist monks of the area. Monks who were not beyond substance abuse and cruelty it seemed. The tigers looked fine, really they did, but they were not. She asked one more time, increasingly impassioned, '*What are you going to do about it?*'

'The world is always changing, things like this never last.' I tried this tack because I didn't want to tell her what happened the last time I tried to intervene.

'Well change it faster, or I will!' she spat out, clearly enraged with my unwillingness to act.

'You'll do more damage than good ... what would you do when you took them out of there?' I asked.

'Put them back where they came from, no animal should be used like that!'

'Lemon, they wouldn't survive, they don't know how to feed themselves anymore, just look at them!' The tigers were kept on thick chains, groomed and fed, electrocuted and drugged. 'You must understand, the people who come to this place only want one thing really - photos.'

In this prison with tickets for admission the monks knew they had to keep up appearances as well as keep the tourists from harm, so they trained the tigers in the way that dangerous killing machines are tamed, through fear and pain. Then, as a precaution, they drugged them with sedatives and tranquilisers. They looked fine. Eyes bright enough. Sometimes they would even walk around.

'Then someone must help them, give them food and freedom,' she seemed adamant that the solution was simple. 'Give them to someone who looks after them.'

'Because dropping sixteen fully grown tigers and twenty cubs on the girl with all the sick cats would work?' I pointed out the flaws in her plan. 'We can't just relocate these huge animals like that.'

'If we don't help them, who will?' Lemon had a point, 'The people don't care.'

'The people would care if they knew ...' I started to build to a point, the point was moot.

'How can they not see this, it's not exactly a secret!' her voice was becoming shriller with each exasperated comeback.

'They don't want to see it, I know it's obvious, but look here,' I zoomed her right in on a sign quite near the tiger temple, it said simply, 'Come and support the tiger sanctuary.'

Lemon curled her upper lip back in disgust, 'They can't just lie like that ...'

'They can! Who's going to stop them?'

'If the visitors find out, they will never come back again,' she refused to budge.

'Do you think the tourists want to know that it's that cruel and painful? No, they want to believe they are doing something good ...'

'It is not hard to see what's going ...'

'They don't want to see it, so they ignore it,' I cut her off in an attempt to finally explain, 'They want a photo with a tiger, they don't want to know the truth or the photo is ruined.'

'You just said they would care if they knew,' Lemon pushed back. 'Now you say they know.'

'Knowing and understanding something is completely different to seeing something but ignoring it because you don't like what you've seen.'

She let out the loudest silence I had ever heard, minutes passed in seconds, I sought for a way out.

Chapter 25 – the offer

Boon looked at Sud and laughed.

'*Kim cut Sud hair*,' Nu sang, finger pointing at me. We had been over it again and again, the whole story and although they now knew what happened, the emphasis was always on me shaving Sud's head.

'Yeah, yeah, okay,' I had heard the joke a few times already.

'Kim?' Boon laughed through his words, looking at me like I had six arms. 'What you do?'

'I cut off all of Sud's hair,' I told him, slightly exasperated.

'Kim?' I just waited for what was next. 'Kim crazy ...'

Why am I the crazy one? Here I am, 22 years old, happy as a clam, pretending I can draw and shaving a meth addict's head at four in the morning. What's crazy about that? Oh!

'Today is the one where you get a shop for Kim.'

I didn't understand, so I parroted, 'Shop for Kim?'

'Shop for Kim,' he said and walked out the door, I guessed I was supposed to follow him. Boon stopped in front of the open shuttered unit next door. The place, which before had been a fish spa, was mostly abandoned, with only a desk and some empty metal frames remaining.

Boon threw his arms open with a flourish to encompass the mostly empty space. 'Kim shop,' he said in wonderment.

'Kim shop?' I had to stop calling myself Kim, 'My shop?'

Boon beamed back at me. 'Open one week okay, mai?' He put one hand on my shoulder and answered himself, 'Yes, Mr. Kim can open one week, Nu work tattoo for you, make big money. Today Kim clean, tomorrow friend me bring two tattoo chair.'

I surveyed my new shop. It was cool and had a fresh feeling that was a rare find in Thailand. The wood-look lining on the floor needed a clean and the water damaged walls had to be painted but it was *my shop*. I already knew what I wanted – this would be the island's first organised, clean and well-lit bamboo-tattoo shop, and it could be a new standard.

I needed to relax and clear my head after a day of cleaning and scraping dirt. With good music in my ears I made my way to the ledge above the island that I had almost hurtled off, and here I planned out the new shop. On a scrap of paper I outlined the area, drawing in some plants on the left and the tattoo chairs in front of them angled towards the street so passers-by could see the work that was being done. I would keep the walls empty and white and buy new strip lights so that the artists could see what they were doing, then add a divide between the eating area and the inking area so the shop part actually looked like a shop.

I made a list of what I needed and added some things that I just wanted; an ice box for fresh beers, some sort of surface cleaner would be great and new cushion cases for the stained torn furniture.

In the morning I would leave the island for the first time in months, and in a few days I would run my own tattoo shop. Well, Boon's tattoo shop - with my name on it, but the freedom was exhilarating.

Chapter 26 – Kim shop

I took a ride on the back of a motorbike taxi, flying through the busy streets with a loaded ice box wedged between myself and the driver. I was still shoeless and my toes clipped the road on corners, the little chicken chaser bike sometimes lost grip for a few heart-stopping moments as it cut corners in-between traffic.

I had to spend a night in the city and tided myself over with a drink with some backpackers, and set out to catch the early morning boat to the island, lugging my haul. The weight of it all was surprisingly heavy - it was a bit of a struggle - and I found myself stopping to sit on the loaded ice-box every five minutes, but I was looking forward to the cool shade and to see everyone again.

I saw them pretty quickly, because they were inside my new shop, seemingly playing a game I could only imagine could be called 'put all the things everywhere' or even 'the less logic, the better!' The place had been well and truly crack-denned too. Sud and Lek were spread eagle over the new tattoo chairs – presumably exhausted after somehow managing to plaster every available newly painted space with assorted print-outs of tattoos. True to form, I could even spot a few celebrities amongst the examples. It might be hard to convince anyone that Angelina Jolie got her famous Cambodian Sak Yant design here. In this shop. The one which had just opened.

Within the twenty-four hours they'd left stir-fried wood maggots on an electric wok with circles of grease soaking through the transfer paper. The usual half-eaten portion of fish on the designing table told me that this chaos probably started the moment I got on that boat. I picked up a few empty beer cans lying against the open box of clean needles and sat down on the sofa, which had been 'welcomingly' turned round to face its back towards the door.

Needless to say, arguments ensued. 'Kim crazy' was quickly becoming my least favourite phrase, but it might have looked like this was true while I was physically trying to sweep Sud, Nu and Bua out of the shop with the floor brush.

It took most of the day to un-Thai-style the place, repainting the long lines of sticky tape that had held up hordes of print-outs, throwing out two of the cushions that had sat in fish juice, tidying, reorganising and cleaning everything up again.

An hour before sunset it was how I wanted it, looking fresh and hygienic - but still with a relaxed atmosphere; the clean needles stored safely away from the food, the beer away from the tattoo chairs and the meth away from the front door.

So I opened my shop right then - I couldn't risk letting the space out of my sight again. Sliding the shutters up and letting in the light, I put on some reggae music and sat back.

It was less than a minute before the first people came in. It was less than an hour before Nu touched the first needle to skin. By full nightfall Lek was working on the second chair and three people sat on the sofa. By midnight the sofa had become a third tattoo bench where Bua was tapping away; the music had turned over to summertime saxophone house and soon after that it was so busy we were telling people to come back tomorrow. I slid the shutters down at sunrise, hid the money in the roof panels and slept in the shop – things were finally looking up.

This went on for *months.* The shop was so full Boon came nightly to collect his half of the money, with the rest going to the artists and the usual cut for me. My percentage was double now as I wasn't sharing, but they seemed to be doing okay next door and any time it was quiet Sud came to work with us.

I started running again; it was something I had been missing in my life recently with all the drinking and working. Visiting my place of solace each time to keep my head straight and appreciate what I had, I could feel myself getting healthier mentally and physically. I didn't even have to worry about my visa anymore; the island was my home and every sunset was better than the last.

Okay *maybe* I was taking a few too many 'diet pills' to keep it all going, but the shop had queues like I hadn't seen on the island before – people would arrive and start asking around for 'Clem's shop.'
Maybe I had found my place. Happy and flying high with the people of the sun.

'It's not that different.'

'It's completely different,' I told her, exasperated, 'they just don't know what they are doing, it happens all over.'

'It's stupidity.'

'It's bad education.'

'They know what's wrong.'

'Yes.'

'They see themselves so much higher than the tigers.'

'Yes.'

'But how?' Lemon jabbed four open fingers towards the earth, 'They are pathetic.'

'Hey! You said they were incredible.'

'No!' she seemed affronted 'This!' jutting her hand again, 'is incredible. Your people are cruel and sadistic.' The people were mean, but to me still fascinating. The way they simply accepted their level as higher than the other living things was a problem, but it was because they had developed in their own way, their technology and the way they communicate. The truth was that most of the living things communicated in their own fascinating way, the people were overcomplicated things. 'I've shown you good people.'

'You've shown me one!'

Not this again, we were running in circles. The girl who fed the cats still sat, kittens between her feet, how many good people would I have to show her before she was convinced. More than one I guess.

'You show me one good person; I'll show you ten evil,' she said, 'then you tell me if this is worth it,'

'Wait? What?' I hope she doesn't mean what I think, 'Not everyone is bad, or good, so many are just, well, neutral.'

'You mean they don't care?'

'They care, they just don't do anything.'

'So they don't care.'

It was a good point, but this was the thing about the people, if they can get away without acting, they won't act. 'Look at the island,' I told her, 'the people aren't bad people, but they aren't stupid.'

'They are,' she said stubbornly.

'No, look. They are just going about their lives, but they know how a place like this can exist,' I had to get through to her somehow, 'people know that there are no rules for a reason.'

'There are laws.'

'Yes, but the corruption is stronger than the law,' maybe she hadn't been paying as much attention as I thought, 'Lemon, people are killed weekly, they know it, everyone knows it, but they love their lives and to challenge the injustice would be to change something that they enjoy.'

'But people are being killed weekly,' she repeated, 'and the people don't do anything about it, *this* means that they aren't good people.'

'People are killed over drugs and money,' I told her, 'it's not directly connected to most people, they aren't bad, they are just good at looking after themselves.'

'People are killed for fun!' Perhaps she had been paying attention, I had been played, 'and for sex, and for money, and for ...'

'Okay!' Guilt twanged again, 'okay!'

'So are these people good?'

'They aren't ...'

She cut in with a tone that stopped me dead in my tracks. 'Correct, they are not!'

'I can do it,' what I was saying was nothing more than batting the ball back at her, 'I could just take the whole failed project and shake it until there was nothing left.'

'They deserve it,' thwack, she smacked back, 'the pain far outweighs the good.'

'This won't take long,' I said, reaching forward as if to completely destroy the earth. She would stop me and the conversation would have to return to reason.

She left it a split-second too late for comfort, as if seriously contemplating not stopping me.

'NO!' she planted a hand on my chest and stopped me dead just short of the cloud bank.

'Why not?' I knew the argument was over, 'the pain far outweighs the good.'

'Killing them all isn't the answer,' she said. I sat back satisfied for a second, until she added, 'we just need to kill the humans.'

'What?!' I was taken aback, 'What, just reach down and squish them one by one?'

'The bad ones, yes.' She truly seemed serious. She was playing to win.

'What do you think would happen if giant fingers just started coming down and killing people?'

'Everyone would be terrified,' she said, quite obviously. 'Then they would see why.'

'Why they were being killed?'

'You do something bad, you get mushed,' she said, matter-of-factly. 'Soon they will work it out.'

'And you really think this would work?' I laughed, doubting my mirth.

'Yes,' she sat back satisfied just like I had a mere thirty seconds ago, before this talk of mass extermination. 'For sure!'

'You know I can't do that, and I know you can't bring yourself to cause that amount of pain'

'No. I can,' she said. I was shocked but still trying to work out if I was being challenged or dealing with a very different Lemon.

'Okay, do one.' My heart suddenly let itself be known, beating up towards my throat. Of course she wasn't about to kill someone? 'Kill a monk,' I egged her on.

'Okay,' she said, rocking onto her knees and theatrically hunting her eyes around the ocean, finding the coast. There it was, thousands of miles below her fingers, the tiger temple, where pain began for so many lives. 'This one!'

Chapter 27 – spirit animals

Lek and Bua, the ambassadors for Team Meth Addiction, popped their heads around the corner, 'Kim you can help, mai? Sud sick.'
Sud was not sick.

Sud was on the floor, growling. Like an animal. Scratching at the walls and drooling. His long nails didn't help the entire scene, nor did the patchy grow-back of his hair and the mad look in his eyes.

'What's this now?' Even after the calm ride I'd been having recently, this level of bizarre was still easy to digest and right now this fully grown man was pretending to be a dangerous cat. Sud looked up and let out a long deep growl – something was definitely not right.

'Sud tiger,' Nu pointed out.

'Oh?' I said, 'That's nice.'
Sud lurched a foot forward, roaring and hissing, swiping with one 'claw'.

'Sud smoke Yaba, mai?' I asked. I was not in the right state of mind for all this, I just wanted to enjoy my day and here is Sud, on the floor, being a tiger.

'Him animal inside him,' Nu explained.

'No, him take too much Yaba,' I interjected.

'Him not take Yaba now,' Lek chimed in unhelpfully.

'That's probably why he's a tiger then, isn't it?' It would either be one or the other.

'Better Sud not work today,' Nu offered.

'You fucking think?!' I snapped - then rolled my eyes towards Sud so Nu knew I wasn't mad at him. The tiger snarled and padded across the room. 'Nope!' I ran forward and blocked him before he stepped out into the street. This man, or tiger, was not about to get away. He looked at my feet, hissing again.

I tried to get him up, he didn't seem dangerous, just deranged and very convinced he was a tiger. I guess he knew tigers walked on all fours, so that's how he insisted on staying. The longer we were here, the more passers-by were noticing and although I wasn't sure what to do I knew I had to get him away from the street and the shops – so I took him by the skin where his neck met his shoulders, and walked him.

Still on all fours, prowling, I steered Sud through the corner of the bar opposite and down the edge of the dry-grass field behind. I tried to take the back roads and found myself heading towards my house.

Sud kept roaring at people who stared too long, I laughed like it was some sort of joke in an attempt to make it look like this wasn't actually a man walking another man like a dog. It didn't work, because that was exactly what was happening.

When we got to my hut I opened the door and channelled him inside, pushing the newly fixed door back into place behind him. Holding it closed with my elbow I pulled a piece of cable from under the edge of the house and for lack of a better idea started to tie the door into the frame.

It was as easy as that, I would leave my home with the door knotted shut and Sud inside. Thinking to myself, 'So this is how it is now - if there's a problem, kidnap it.' It worked. As I walked away from the house, although I could hear him making circles and scratching at the bamboo, I just didn't care. The morning was good, then something annoying happened, and now it's gone. Not normal no, but maybe this was the new normal though, considering the tiger and the kidnap, I felt very much in control of the day.

'We should think about this,' she hesitated, two fingers in the atmosphere, 'Are you sure?'

'I am not, you are,' I made my stance known, the tiny monk stood behind a red rope his hand stretched out to accept more Thai Baht as tourists filed past.

'If I do this, everything changes.'

I knew Lemon wouldn't be able to do it. Well, apart from that one moment when I thought she was about to. The monk held up his hand to indicated maximum capacity and stood back, still alive. 'You don't have to.'

'I want to.'

'Everyone wants to,' I told her, 'when they pay too much attention to the truth.'

'What if I'm wrong?'

'Exactly, and then he would be dead and you would be the bad one.'

'Okay ...' she hesitated but her fingers had unwittingly inched back already. 'We won't start now.'

'Okay,' I agreed.

'But we will start one day, if nothing changes.'

'Okay.'

'Like you said it would.'

I wanted to contend how my words had been twisted a little, but right now the annihilation was postponed so I went with, 'Yes, if nothing changes.'

'Tomorrow,' she decided.

'That's just two years,' I pointed out, 'for them.'

'Yes, two years of pain and suffering,' she noted, 'then they start to die.'

'Just the bad ones, yes,' I reminded her, and then negotiated, 'let's give them five.'

Chapter 28 – organised chaos

I stood close to the front door and listened but I heard no growls or scratching. No four limbs trampling around in circles. I had slept in the shop after another day of record sales; this also meant Sud had been in his cage for 24 hours. I was in a good place and this drug addled tiger was a problem, but this is the power of the 'Island Eyes'. This solitude way of pretending a problem is nothing, just to preserve your contentment in life, to the point that you think about it in the same way as you think about a door handle, for a split second until the door is open and you can breeze right through, still, at some point I would have to let him out.

I struggled with my two minds, and finally said out loud, 'Sud?'

No noise. I pried the cable out of the knot and let it spring away, holding the door in the frame with my elbow again, the prospect of opening this door to check on my friend fought against the small part of me that was telling me to walk away, it had been a great day and opening this door can only bring drama. 'What was I thinking?' I checked myself, I was increasingly disturbed that I didn't think twice about locking him in, now I was thinking about leaving him there. It was easy but I knew it wasn't right.

I took my elbow away and let it emit the familiar 'krumpf' noise as it slid off the base of the frame. With two fingers I guided it back, standing to one side and after a few seconds of nothing, peered into the gloom. Sud lay there, awake, on the completely unmade mattress. The sheets had been strewn all over and the few possessions I had scattered with them. His arms were propping him up folded by his sides.

'Kim, what time?' he asked, scrunching up his eyes. 'Morning, now I go to work,' I said, scanning the room and assessing the damage. There were things I would fix later but I was willing to let this all blow over, it was an easy option in the light and clarity of a new day.

Back at the shop it was all going on. I didn't have a chance to talk to anyone about the whole 'tiger thing' or the disappearance of Sud, with ten or more customers waiting I was bombarded with questions:

'Can you look me in the eye and tell me the needles are new for each tattoo?'

'Yes, because I hold them.'

'Kim what is Ser-pent?'

'Big snake.'

'Hey man, this is your place? I need...'

'Kim want beer, mai?'

Finally a question I wanted to hear 'Yes!'

We had a new artist, I don't know how. Bua just introduced him as 'Sai' with 'him work here okay'. He looked like Lek but with no moustache. Sai had actually dragged an old gym bench up the street and into the shop, throwing a sarong over it and then adding his name to the books.

Compared to the pirate-style living quarters of the other shops around, any tattoo artist who was ready to take his work seriously would likely turn up at the door, so the worry about drugs and tigers faded into the back of my brain and I got back to enjoying the moment. How could one place be so simple yet so complicated?

Sud came in a few hours later, he wasn't a tiger anymore and nobody else seemed too tweaked right now. Maybe it was just a thing that happens with meth now and again, it was nothing that a quick kidnapping didn't fix and now everything seemed fine. The music was relaxed and the beer was cold, the shop was full and the floor was clean.

It was hard to split the customers from the spectators as they all lined up together, waiting and bustling and talking about their next tattoo, even Thai locals were popping in to see what was going on. The troughs were easy to ignore when the peaks were so high.

In the midst of this organized chaos, as I sat back in the only available chair surveying the scene with a smile, a face appeared directly in my line of sight, something familiar tugged at my memory but for the life of me I couldn't place it. The stranger had glided into view; stopping his bike with a grinding halt in front of my shop and fixing me with this dead-pan stare, his mouth thin and relaxed. It lasted only a second or two, his eyes didn't flicker at all as one hand reached up, extended the index finger and drew a slow line across his own neck.

I didn't notice I'd been holding my breath until I let it out – it was a death threat! My Island Eyes fought to ignore this, and lost – my contentment shattered so soon after it had been rebuilt, settling as shards in the pit of my stomach.

The crab – episode 4

A crab's world has several dimensions. It can walk on the top of a flip-flop, much like people do – but seeing as he is a crab all eight feet fit on half the sole. He can walk sideways around the edge, a dimension only for the most agile of humans. A crab can also walk on the bottom of the flip-flop, upside down and, for this particular crab, under the water.

This crab was doing just this, casually standing upside down, feeding on the algae that formed a beard hanging below his boat.

Things were good, that storm was long done and the algae tasted fine. It was cool and comfortable in the shade down here and just as he was thinking about taking another bite a huge shadow soared under, or over, his head. 'What the hell was that!?' The wake from whatever-it-was pushed him sideways and shook the whole ship. The thing, formally known as some sort of barracuda, turned and as it did - its teeth turned with it.

The crab bolted, wrapping his pointy feet around the edge he hoisted himself up onto the dry side of the sole. The shoe shook again, more violently this time; the crab hoped this was curiosity not hunger as he pulled all eight legs to the centre of the flop hoping it didn't flip.

This is where he stayed, for maybe another two hours, after all, where could he go? A crab in the middle of the ocean didn't have as many options as he once did, and now he had 50% less safe space than he thought he did before. The light was fading when he finally crept to the edge of the foam, his heart in his throat, hoping against hope that the monster had left. His eyes adjusted to a new shape, meters below him, sliding through the deep was a second shadow, much bigger than a barracuda. It wasn't getting closer, it was hovering. Just metres away - a deep sliver in a blackening sea.

Chapter 29 – the longest night

I looked out into the almost empty midnight street, cleared by the recent rain. Almost, apart from one of the girls from the massage shop down the road, hurtling towards us appearing and disappearing in the glow emitted from street lights and shop windows. When she got to the shop she stepped around me and went right inside to speak to Bua and Lek, I already knew this was bad news by their knee jerk reaction, springing up in that 'somebody's going to get hurt' style of bravado.

They left, she followed, Sud stayed behind but the new guy Sai was nowhere to be seen. I hesitated, and then reluctantly gave chase. The three of us got to the end of the street at the same time and inside the shop was a very drunk man shouting and kicking the furniture. He had that egg-head look going on and his formerly white clothes were grubby and stretched from an obviously big night. His temper was definitely not that of someone who had just reached climactic release, as he explained loudly that he had paid for a hand job and he had been robbed.

This was quite possible, the trick with the drunk-blackout guys who took too long, was to squirt lube or moisturiser on them and convince them that it had all gone to plan.

The man turned to me, perhaps assuming I was another tourist trying to intervene, with, 'What the fuck you looking at?'

Oops! Lek and Bua didn't need a translator for the word 'fuck' or for the man's tone. Mistake number two came a second later, as he swiped his trunk like arm across in front of him, clearing one of the girls right out of his path and crashing her against the door. Tension was in the air, and as he made his way to exit I had a flicker of thought that this might end okay and maybe we were just here to make sure he left quickly and didn't hurt anyone.

Two steps away from the shop he turned, protruded his sweating face towards Lek and Bua, and said, very clearly, 'Fuck ... Off!'

That was mistake number three, and still not something they needed me to translate due to the overly enunciated nature of the delivery. The Yaba, that sat in the pit of their psyche cracked open an eye.

'Oh by all the gods not again,' I said to myself as I watched Lek reach into his belt where he kept his blade. The man showed them a middle finger over his own shoulder as he burst into the street, pausing for a moment as if this had put him off balance, and then swayed side to side with each step as he started again up the road.

None of this was good news because most of all Ya didn't like her hosts being insulted, either that or she relished in the excuse to kick-start her own brand of problem solving; predictably they followed, presumably to cut that finger clean off.

The distance they left between themselves and the man was disconcerting enough for me to feel the need to catch up and keep between them - I had seen it all before and knew they were just waiting for him to leave the safety of the main street.

Lek put his left arm around me as the other already held his duct-tape-handled weapon out in the open, 'Him not good man,' he told me, making a lazy 'z' in the air with the pointy end. My brain groaned, 'Just give me one day without murder or tigers.'

To the mental swagger of a meth-addled man a few stabs with a knife isn't the worst thing in the world, but from the recent experience with the fool and a bike, I knew that it wouldn't easily stop there, and to kill a man over the equivalent of thirty dollars would be hard to forget.

We followed him for a few more minutes, he was painfully unaware that he was about to get stabbed to death in an alleyway so my heart sank as he took a lazy left down a side street.

Lek prepared to interrupt his stroll, turning the blade inside his hand to face downwards and dropping it so the spike ended inches from his palm. This was going to be messy. I knew I had to help the man. This idiot was about to screw everything up for all of us but I knew getting between a meth addict and his tunnel vision wasn't the best idea - not if you wanted to keep your own eyes anyway. Maybe I can accidentally let this guy know he's being followed ... and then maybe he's smart enough to get away by himself?

I scanned the half-built surroundings and saw a cut-off scaffold pole, maybe half a meter long. I picked it up roughly by one end making sure the other clanked onto the road; it made a slight noise - but nothing that overtly, yet subtly, said, 'You are being followed and will likely be stabbed,' so that plan didn't work at all.

Keeping the pole with me and still half unsure what I was going to do with it, I thought about how this would look to a bystander. I scoped the street again and noted with relief that there was still nobody around. I looked at my pole and Lek's knife; both caught the moonlight in the wrong way.

'I want to do it,' came out of my mouth as I brandished my makeshift weapon. I figured, out of the two options, this would have a better outcome.

'Together,' came the drug addled reply. Great, so now I've gone from witnessing murder to assisting it, well done Clem. 'Tattoo boys mafia boys,' Lek said.

The man heard this and he turned around with a quick, 'Fuck off fuuuuuck offffffff.' This time I sensed less bravado in his voice.

The space between us closed far too quickly. 'Stop saying fuck please.' I hissed. I was running out of options and a human life seemed to be worth nothing out here.

The man seemed to have sensed danger at last, he stopped and stood with his side facing us, but still he wasn't running? Maybe it was a good thing as we were half surrounding him now and the chase would have just excited Ya. She would have relished in making this into a hunt with a bloody ending.

Before anyone else could act I swung the scaffold pole and hit the man in the back of the head. The pole let out a hollow ring from its colliding end and with a dull grunt he dropped to his knees and landed flat. My mind raced; too much? This is the moment I really hoped he wasn't dead.

Lek looked at me, the tension ballooned out of the scene and he just looked impressed. 'Kim baa,' he said with slight awe. In English, it means, 'Clem is crazy,' I heard this all too often in recent days and was slowly coming into agreement.

We looked down at the guy as I mentally projected trying to somehow penetrate the dull unconscious lump, 'Don't get up … be alive, but don't get up.' I threw the pole into some crumpled tarpaulin in an effort to present an end to the attack and Lek, now not faced with a moving target, followed suit and tucked the knife.

I didn't look back.

Chapter 30 – human life

It was hard, forgetting the night before, but every dark moment was a divide in the path of life. A choice for who you wanted to be, it had gotten out of hand but still the sun rose as it always did and nobody seemed any different.

The worth of human life still got to me – or rather the lack of it. We had all shared in what happened on the street though, having snuck back to remove the weapon from the side of the road, I knew the man had regained consciousness and left, but there was no doubt that this hadn't been their objective. Yet there was nothing to talk about and that was my problem, we were so far down this rabbit hole that the morality of attacking a man with a knife, or a pipe, wasn't even mentioned the next day.

There was something wrong with this. In a society that claims the name 'Land of Smiles' and an outlook on life other than personal wealth, there was a tendency to kill someone for less worth than the land under their feet. Or, I guess, simply because your meth-addled brain excited you into it.

'Watch your back save your life,' the woman spoke quickly and with intent as she passed through my daydream daze drifting down Beach road. I didn't respond, from my glance back at her walking away I knew who she was; she worked at one of the smallest shops right at the end of the main tattoo street. I swallowed the lump before it reached my throat, I was safe, I knew that - I had some protection from the 'organisation' I had found myself part of. My mental state, however, was struggling with what that meant too.

My reaction was much the same as it always has been when confronted with a moral conundrum, or a peak of stress, I found an outlet, seeking out a moment to eclipse the underlying issues and push them out of mind. Usually I fuck or I run. Today I ran, taking the old well-worn jungle path to my jungle platform of solace.

The condensation trail from a rising aeroplane stole light from above the low laying cloudbank, burning a red scar across the sky. Someone was going somewhere - I had been on this island for so long that just the thought of check-ins and baggage limits touched a small anxiety in my chest. The world which I always fought to avoid seemed to spread everywhere outside of these hills, but when I thought back to the moment when I first ran this track and let the green replace the grey; I felt the same anxiety push up inside me.

I should have trusted my gut, something felt wrong. I walked back down the track as the sun slid away, reaching the shop before the light left the sky completely.

Chapter 31 – okay mai?

'Kim, yes?' it was Gan, the owner of the first tattoo shop at the top of the road, 'Kim okay, mai?'

'Yeah, Kim okay,' I lied, of course I had a lot on my mind, 'You okay, mai?'

'No Kim, Gan not okay,' Gan shook his head, putting an arm around my shoulders as he continued, 'Kim we can talk something?' It wasn't really a question as the arm around me tightened and steered me with him out of the shop. Sud sat in the back of the unit, I looked back at him for a sign but maybe Sud had avoided my eye, or was genuinely not looking in my direction, I felt like it were the former.

We walked, or rather, Gan led me, to another tattoo shop just a little further down the road, it wasn't his own shop but they ran in the same circles and shared artists quite often – Sai worked with them before he join us. Once inside Gan released his grip but it was obvious I wasn't free.

The owner, a man I knew by reputation as a nice enough guy, cleared the couch and retreated to the back of his own store. Gan then indicated for me to sit on this couch, his expression somewhat calm but not to be disagreed with, I sat. Crouching and planting himself on a small stool in front of me Gan emitted a dominant position even from this lower level. He spoke 'Mr Kim, I like you,' then exhaled as if this was a relief to him.

I said nothing, knowing this wasn't what he had brought me here to tell me.

'But,' he continued, 'You will never work in tattoo again okay?'

I should have seen this coming. 'I work for Boon.'

Gan's facial expression didn't change, but his eyes did. He reached into his waistband, just as Lek had done the night before, and took a short sharp knife out of his Marley-pants. Another exhalation, this time not one of relief. Gan reached his other hand out and onto the side of my face, fingers on my cheek and a thumb on my chin, then his entire body tensed slamming the back of my head hard into the wall above the chair. That knife came fast towards my face and found its way effortlessly into my open mouth, stopping just above my tongue. I could smell the metal above all other senses. 'Okay?' he asked one more time.

'Ooaaay,' I tried to agree with his point of view, without touching a blade that I assumed had been used before.

'If Gan see you work tattoo, Kim no more.' It was more disconcerting that he didn't even look angry.

I tried to nod without dying and Gan exhaled and an even more relaxed look spread over his face. 'Okay Kim!' He withdrew both arms, popping to his feet and walking out.

I sat in silence, shell-shocked. I didn't need to think about it, I just had to do what I was told.

Sud knew what was up before I was inside the door.

'Kim okay?'

'Tell Boon the shop is not mine,' I told him. The shop stayed silent as I took the empty ice box and threw any of my things I could see into it. I walked out and into the dark, through the dry field and to my house. I dropped the box right inside the door and the smell of urine from where the tiger had peed in the corner swelled into my nostrils, anything was better than the stench of that blade. I didn't go inside but pushed the door back into place and turned back into the night. Somehow I felt safer than before; now that I knew that it had all been leading up to this.

The street shook from diet pills and mixed liquor as I left the bar, everyone seemed to be travelling in the opposite direction, faceless and grinning. Blink. That was a mistake, the blink twisted the world, a split second of sickness and a stumble. Someone was behind me, following me, I was sure. Far too much drink and the pungent smoke of the room had made this feeling a small hell. I sped up. The people were passing too close, maybe they knew something I didn't, I took a rogue left to shake whoever it was off my tail. 'I'm out, I don't work in tattoos, what's this about?' Each step landed hard on my front foot as I turned out of the detour towards home. Pain, as my knee caught the edge of a raised pallet platform holding promotional signs, I turned to see what it was I had hit and lost balance, veering into a shutter – the noise was never ending. I lurched away from it into a half run. There was this clatter from behind, like something I had knocked down or something being picked up? My consciousness lagged and flickered in a twisted haze when I found myself by my own door, looking back one last time, face to face with nobody at all. The door gave way at a lean and with two steps and a trip I felt the bed like wet sand. My mind and stomach spun wildly in opposite directions.

Chapter 32 – hand in hand

Pain tore beneath my eyelids, I screwed them tight shut against the light that had flooded the room with my door dropping away from its frame. I was still drunk, my lips unpeeled from each other and the taste of gin and mouth-breathing mingled with the hard ache of a dehydrated brain.

That creak meant the door had been pulled to, but not all the way. My brain picked though murky memories in reverse, I recalled the walk home, Gan's eyes, that ringing noise as the metal pipe connected with that guy's head. I heard my eyes open, Boon had chosen not to sit this time, I didn't blame him, the smell of ammonia was still pungent in the air from days before. I checked the covers were covering, only to find myself fully clothed. The other arm didn't move, I found it underneath me, cut numb.

'Kim not work today?'

I just lay there, my head too heavy to lift out of the sweat-damp pillow, pins and needles filled my arm as the blood slowly returned. The light shone thin strips and spikes through the damaged thatch casting dots and dashes onto the bedding. Drifting dust particles caught the light to create an almost vertical cage effect around me. This told me it was past midday already, pausing to swallow dry nothing I managed seven words, 'I'm not going to die for money.'

Boon grinned, were his teeth always this white? They shone in the dim light but it was far from a soothing smile. 'Kim not worry,' he didn't ask why, but the island was small.

I was feeling brave with my words - it might have

been the alcohol. 'Clem does worry when he has a knife in his mouth,' just saying it turned my stomach with memory of the stained blade on my tongue, I repeated a shortened less menacing version of Gan from the night before, 'Kim not work tattoo,'

Boon was still smiling, I wished I could properly make out his expression, to read something in his eyes and not just that manic grin. 'Boon speak Gan,' he told me carefully, 'have no problem, can work tattoo okay.'

'He said he would kill me.' I was adamant that this was a big deal, Boon sighed and leant down very awkwardly patting my knee, some fresh bruising made itself known.

'Kim! Boon big boss okay.'

I raised my head a fraction of an inch. Dealing with a hangover had become common practice but the amount of alcohol you can get through when you thought that you were about to be murdered and then you're not, this wasn't something I had much experience in. 'I can't work today, feel sick.'

Boon had once seen me on my way to work still half-drunk holding a dislocated arm, so he knew a hangover wasn't the reason. 'Kim not be scared, go new shop one hour, mai?'

'I'm not scared!' I was scared. Of course I was but I was also hungry, stupid and easy persuaded. 'Okay,' I nodded my head, the room nodded around me a second later, my stomach performed a backflip and in a clumsy scramble I passed the big boss' legs and projected several mouthfuls of vomit through the gap below the door.

I swallowed the taste, Boon left me with my head half out of the entrance and even though I couldn't look up I heard him cycle away and pulled the door back into darkness. My skin reeked of stale beer, sweat or vomit dropped from my chest and every logical thought that ran through my mind took me to somewhere distressing. Breathing deeply I let myself give in to a surreal tangent - maybe just maybe, none of this was actually happening. It had gone too far to be real. I pondered the idea of accepting this delusion, maybe it was me that was taking it all too hard and life was just like this.

My mind on the fence I decided to go forward with caution and hedonism hand in hand, I wouldn't back down so easily, but I would speak to Gan and make sure that wide white smile was genuine.

I only needed one item of clothing, my shorts, and just like that I was almost ready for the day. I couldn't find my toothbrush so I filled my mouth with toothpaste and rubbed it around with a finger. It wasn't the first time this week. I spat the foam into a bush halfway into town and spat once more into my hand before rubbing it into my hair. It wasn't glamorous but it tamed the fluffy sticky-out bits. Looking down I could tell I had crossed paths with some sharp objects on the way home last night because sand had stuck to the dried blood around my toes; the same could be said for one knee, the opposite shin and both palms.

So back to work, right? I knew something wasn't really okay, the acceptance had come far too quickly. I was still feeling brave when I walked a different route to work and accidentally on purpose found the man who had put a knife in my mouth last night. Gan sat Thai-style in the sand outside his tattoo shop, working on the design display stands with a handheld circular grinder, letting a fountain of sparks arch from where the blade guard had been removed allowing the embers to shower into the street, forcing passers-by to take a small detour. I watched and waited until the last of the sparks bounced away and the grindstone wail had spun to a stop. Gan looked up. 'Hello Kim.' He didn't seem angry, he didn't seem anything.

'Gan everything okay?' I asked in an attempt at an offhand manor.

'Yes Kim,' He replied calmly. Relief ebbed into my anxiety.

'So it's okay I work tattoo now?'

In a second Gan's eyes went wild and wide, his face changed into an aggressive contort and he spat angrily at me, 'Fuck! Kim want die already?'

'Okay, okay, I not work tattoo okay?' I blurted out, backing away.

This time Gan didn't soften his expression; he didn't speak at all. He just stared at me as if I was the crazy one. I could still feel his eyes on the back of my head as I walked past my shop on his way to the beach. 'Kim, Kim!' Bua called to me from behind the sample display. I shook my head quickly and just kept walking.

Anger welled up inside me for the first time in a long time, I walked away, my mind flitting through quick resolves to my problems, like floating over this island like a blimp reaching down and twisting his neck around.

I understood Gan, well I understood his need to protect his livelihood, but Boon! I took comfort envisioning a single blow crushing him into the sand, was my life worth just a few extra days profit? The satisfaction of replacing the feeling of helplessness with aggressive resolve occupied my mind all the way to the end of the beach.

I sat where I first sat, which seemed like a lifetime ago, when I let the island wash over me and felt truly disconnected from the outside world. This place reminded me of simpler times, in the shade, at the end of the beach, where days could be whiled away in the breeze without a thought or a care.

Chapter 33 – no problem

'Kim I buy you gun.'

'I don't want one, who am I going to shoot?' I shook my head and stepped back from Boon, it was becoming painfully obvious that he would make excuses and cook lies right up until the day I 'disappeared' and then I would be nothing.

It was something I had noticed about the island; killing someone was incredibly easy and disposing of a body was common knowledge. A corpse in the jungle wouldn't last more than a few days and with so many metres of python gliding around the undergrowth something out there would eventually swallow it whole.

Better yet for would-be murderers, if a corpse did show up in public the police were so desperate to preserve the façade of paradise that they would be more than happy to write it down as a suicide anyway.

'No problem,' Boon gave up quickly, for about ten seconds. 'Kim have bodyguard have gun.' Wow, how much was I worth to this guy? I was taken aback and yes, although a small part of me found it kind of cool, it was a very bad idea.

I presented him with my final decision, tentatively saying, 'I'm sorry Boon, and thanks, but I can't work tattoo anymore.'

Boon nodded, 'Boon have friend who have work for Kim.'

'What kind of work?' I brightened up; I had recently counted my spare change and knew I had around two days of food in my pocket.

He was squirming suspiciously, 'Take something from Burma, easy for farang people'

'Yaba?' It was worded like a question but I already knew the answer.

'Little Yaba little...'

'No!' It was almost funny; I wasn't going to become a drug smuggler, not today anyway. I repeated, with a definite tone, 'No.'

Boon tried one more time in the way that usually worked for him, 'Big money.'

'I don't even have a visa,' I laughed with my mouth only, veering into a subject that had been on my mind.

'You not have visa?' He asked me incredulously.

'What?' I had to be sure he was being serious, 'You told me P-Nai could give me visa.'

Boon shook his head, 'Kim stay too long already,' he opened his hands in the international symbol for, 'what can I say kid?'

'Wait, P-Nai can fix this ...' I felt the adrenaline and desperation crack into my voice as my resolve slipped away.

Boon shook his head again. 'P-Nai not help now, Kim work too long. Need work speak Boon okay?'

Chapter 34 – the secret ingredient is delusion

I am six days into just white rice and milk, swallowing mouth sludge for sustenance. I ignore a small shame that plays on my mind; things that my family might think about me risking it like this. My mother, ever the worrier, my father, even my brothers – they'd care – and the careful risk-free upbringing that somehow led to this. Why is their help so far from my reach? It's not, I am far from it. By now, mentally, I was going somewhere and I had to see it through. Black spots had been playing in the corners of my eyes for some time now.

I put my rice on a tab, the market vendor furrowed her brow but let it slide one more time saying, 'You now give 120 baht next time okay?'

It wasn't okay, but something was exhilarating about the situation and this self-education. In a basic hierarchy of human needs you see that when one need is satisfied your brain looks for the next. It's a pyramid from simply surviving - shelter, water and food - all the way up to drugs, silk and sex. The idea of one-way travel, to relocate to another country from where you had it all, to a place where you are fighting each day, this goes against all human instinct. Here I am now - trying to justify this.

I drank from a half bottle of water that had been left on the beach. I thought about those could-be traveller souls who ignored that voice that whispers *what if* and stayed in the grey zone. Were they better off than me right now? A hard question to argue from both sides. My mind also went to the travellers who came so far only to turn back and realised that the consequence of this is not just nothing, but nothingness. This was my rational for being here; I chose to be here under the relentless sun letting the last warm drips hit my tongue, wondering how much of each drop evaporated in the searing space between the bottle and my mouth.

So where am I now, am I free? I was accepting some truths that I have played with my entire life. You are just another animal. You are not here for a reason, and its unlikely life will give you one. You shouldn't think you are owed anything – least of all happiness, you need to seek that out yourself. Finally I had to admit that this line of thought was summed up by one sentence: I was not inherently set on a path; rather, I was born. From that point on every action has been a choice, my choice. This realization was strangely comforting.

In my hunger and my delusion I couldn't complain. The right to complain is invalid for those who don't change their surroundings. A headache was setting in. Without a valid visa and sitting in wake of Boon's lies, for the first time the border around me had become very real. Right now I was 'safely' on the island, but one step off this spit of sand I would become a fugitive to a harsh Thai penal system; any further afield, I would meet international border control.

A lump in my throat had found itself, but not because of fear but because of frustration. Frustration that all these things were just... *made up by someone one day*, and now these were the things that limit everything we do or see or experience. The law, the working week, the line between France and Spain –

they're not *really* there, unless you accept them. Somehow, at some point, we all did.

I was losing my mind a little in this thought train that seems so obvious at the time that you wonder why this isn't how you always lived. I don't even remember lying down. The sun slapped lethargic layers upon my bare skin, I squinted down the beach. Why are people running?

I stared harder at the figures, through the swimming heat haze I could make out hundreds of shimmering shapes surging in the same direction, my primal brain knew what fleeing looked like. I forced myself into focus and tuned into my surroundings again, the distant but screeching alarm bells of the Tsunami warning rang clear across the island, the sound of death approaching.

A bump of adrenaline surged into my limbs, there it is, that survival instinct, giving me what I needed to run.

I didn't.

I didn't know why but I chose to wait little longer, wait until the people were almost out of sight, then I would follow, I told myself. From what I could make out nobody even looked back. Ten left, then four. Then I was alone on the beach, admiring the sand stretching from my feet to the foot of the mountain. The alarm bells screaming that death was on its way didn't reach me in the same terrifying way as the ones before, not this time ... instead it was possibly exciting?

Blink.

One deep breath and then another. I shook my head in disbelief; never in my life had I felt so adrift but something about every second I waited made me feel a little closer to how I first felt when I arrived on the island. Potential, uncertainty.

The tiny black holes in the bamboo huts that lined the far end of the beach flickered in the rising air. Twenty minutes passed and the warning bells rang on, they were the only thing cutting through the emptiness of the island.

'Everyone must be in the mountains by now, everyone except for me.' I looked at the sea, looking for the tell-tale signs; before a tidal wave the sea would suck out the water out and then it would all come back tenfold and hundred-speed.

The walk to Beach road felt like walking between vicious beasts straining at rusted chains, and I revelled in it. Leaving grooves in the empty sand I picked my way between the abandoned patchworks of towels near the opening to the town, paying attention on taking my time the moment was absolutely meditative – fighting my flight instinct with every careful step.

Wild-West style, the whole place was a ghost town, shimmering in the heat. I looked left and right as I made my way between the storefronts lining the street. This funnel is what would become a smashed tornado of salt water and loose debris if the tsunami did hit.

A clatter came from inside the bar. 'Hello?' I called. A cat had knocked a straw broom down as it ran out of the bar and into my old tattoo shop. When I drew level with the shop and the bar opposite I lingered near a half glass of juice, a full wine and a fruit shake standing beside a cooling Pad Thai. I didn't sit when I squeezed a lemon slice over the untouched dish and twisted a plastic fork into the noodles. The first bite you can imagine was almost too good, as was the second. The banana shake cooled my core as I tried to identify a second ingredient. My eyes then settled on the glass of red wine, it was gone in three gulps. This didn't feel a lot like imminent death. It tasted delicious.

I felt the nutrition awaken my body and I righted an abandoned bicycle that lay on the hot sand between the bar and the road, and letting my bare feet push hard on the pedals I became a moving Clem. Hurtling around the town, audibly whooping and skidding to a halt by a bacon sandwich I claimed it for my own in two bites. I met another cat, slinking by the beer garden's corner table as I finished two half pints and some sort of cocktail. I made it as far as the pier road - it had been left as a Tetris of suitcases where new arrivals had got a welcome that they would never forget.

I sped on my two wheels down long empty roads, turning corners in the knowledge that the street was clear. Just myself and the heat. Smoke rose from a few burning sticks on the beach where I stopped to re-hydrate from someone's water bottle, it was half full and half warm but I wasn't dead so I didn't care.

There is a moment that sailors call a slack tide, the point between the water rising and falling when it isn't going in or out. I watched the taxi boats clack together in the calm, feeling real food bring me back to a conscious level and the water filling my cells again. The alarm ceased in that second, it concluded the symphony to what has taken position as one of the most epic and surreal moment of my entire life.

Chapter 35 – forced minimalism

Life gives and takes.

The balance seemed off. Turning the corner I saw these things in this order;

One heaped pile of thatch - loose pink twine wrapped around it

One migrant worker leaning on a mattock

Two sheets of woven wood - lying flat into the dirt

One white and blue ice box - much like my own

Two men - one with a long-arm hammer and one with a log

Two standing walls,

Half a roof and half a porch - which was becoming less of a porch with each hammer swing.

I wondered how long it took them to completely dismantle my house.

Dow's house still stood, empty with the door wide open. The mattress propped against the wall outside. What had I missed? Where had everyone gone?

The ice box, of course, was mine, the six things inside it were still there with the kind addition of the shorts that had been loose on the floor but now stuffed into the handle. I walked around the scene avoiding swinging hammers and such like, nobody looked twice when I took the box.

I had reached a new level of dazed and confused, wandering back and forth and watching the deconstruction for a while, until Dow's house took its first hammer thump. Thinking about the things I had lost along the way I added an entire family who just upped and left.

The forced minimalism was liberating in its own way - I was down to seven items including what I wore. The three-quarter lengths I had bought to replace the ones swapped with Boon were fairly grimy but still cleaner than the shorts. This toothbrush had seen better days and the tooth paste was reaching the half-way mark. One t-shirt that hadn't been re-appropriated by the tattoo-shop boys and one half bottle of fairy liquid for face/body/dish/hair –the seventh was the box they sat in.

The beach was long and the sand was hot, sweat was dripping from my elbows as I shade-hopped down a route I knew well - it would take me to that spot by the palms where I felt so alive many months before. The washed-up trash from the storm still stuck out of the sand, mostly blown off boats or balconies; paradise didn't look so fresh now. I sat on my ice box in the shade where the beach met the jungle, a nice spot of solitude with barely any litter apart from a few bottles and a rice bag.

I focused on the sun shining on the water, the music carried in the breeze, trying to recall that feeling. Come-on I need this, just a moment of that rush of new beginnings and potential - it seemed that a life bump was a gateway drug and this paradise wasn't strong enough to give me the fix I was looking for. Pop! The lid of the ice box inverted under my weight, dropping me down a few centimetres and putting an abrupt end to my forced mental restart. I jumped off opened the top so I could pop it back into shape but the whole thing came apart at the hinges where it had split through sun, wear and over use.

Searching for some twine or a rope to thread through the hinges I picked up the discarded rice bag and was just about try and strip some bits of the mesh plastic when I changed my mind. The bag was whole, more or less, and clean enough for my dirty clothes - in went the five items. I bunched the top up and threw it over my shoulder, good enough!

So-long ice box, you were good to me when I had beer to fill you with, but you've out-grown me or I've in-grown you – I don't know. I put it down by the long-tail boats, knowing that the fishermen would find a use for it quite quickly - it's the island way of recycling.

Chapter 36 – old friends

By spending time with the few tourists who made it through the rain; sleeping, eating and breathing - I was drinking enough water to sweat and build up enough energy to start looking for work. Life had been worse.

smack something collided with the side of my head. Spitting a mouthful of water and dropping the bottle, I turned around, surprise delayed the pain. There he stood, seething, glaring and covered in tattoos - the same local with the dead eyes that had slid his finger across his neck outside the shop. 'Yooooou!' he hollered. The familiarity in his face was his outline – I made the connection from many months before, one of three silhouettes in the mouth of Beach road attacking the lone girl.

smack, smack he swung two more fists, both connected.

The shop, Gan's shop, wasn't far away and figures stood in the opening. I definitely couldn't hit back, if I did I would have six guys beating me senseless. This would pretty much happen to any westerner who hit back at a Thai man.

smack

'Ow! What?' I asked, the pain from the first punches finally getting through to me.

'I say you, I know you!' the spitting man raged.

'What?! ...' I started, then I saw it. The man was obviously Yabba'd out of his brain, the crazy eyes darting all over my face, the vein in his neck pumping.

This happened when meth soaked your psyche and burnt holes in your recent memory – the chances were that the anger he felt before was still very current when he was this messed up and violence was always the answer when Yaba was the influencer.

'Want die?!' he screamed.

'No, look ...' *a swing and a miss* The little man was fumbling around in his trousers, just like Gan before he drew his knife. This time out came brass knuckles. Ah shit!

'Hey, no, look I'm leaving!' I said, stepping back. The maniac, who may have woken out of his haze for a second, seemed happy that I was backing away, lowered the fist with the knuckleduster and pointed a quivering finger at my face.

'I not want see you here!'

It was enough 'screw it, I'm out,' I told myself, backing up the street. With good ten metres between us the angry little man felt himself victorious and with a last maniacal stare he turned and swaggered away back to his shop.

So - a revelation, I needed a place to lay low for a while until whatever I had done this time was a little further in the past, lest I collect a few extra holes in my face.

My immediate problem was that this island was really the only place I could find work without my visa or a huge bribe, but the catch was, that without these things I couldn't have gone anywhere else, anyway. More importantly, I didn't want to go anywhere, I was happy here. Well apart from those few violent drug addicts, and the knives, and the corruption.

Chapter 37 – Shangri-La

This island wasn't merely a landmass dictated by where it rose from the ocean, but also the smoke that drifted from the fires, the clouds sitting above the twin peaks and the bustle of the sea life surrounding it. Not the ocean creatures, but the ocean people – scuba divers, fishermen, taxi boats and sightseeing trips poured from the port daily, still very much part of the ecosystem that made the island life – it looked to me like a great place to lay low.

I asked around the bars, avoiding the tattoo hotspots and shady alleyways. I needed work away from the thick of it all, a new experience maybe, and someone who cared more about who you are and not what you've done - all fingers pointed to one man.

Dennis was in many aspects a pirate. Sixty three years into a life of adventures and wives, he had sailed his yacht to the Thai islands in search of more good times.

His boat was a 20 metre long sailing yacht made of steel with a teak deck, twin masts and a few cabins. Through a life of use and abuse the mechanicals needed constant maintenance, especially after the rough wet winter that had just hit the coast.

Dennis had bolted some pirate worthy additions onto various places, namely a 20 metre rope-swing that came from the top mast and a three metre arm that folded out from the port side, where it sat just above water level dragging a large thick net behind it, big enough for a party of people to lounge in as the boat cruised between the islands.

Dennis and Nate, a close friend and business partner, planned on refitting and refurbishing the boat ready for the coming high season, where they would take groups out on day trips, drinking, snorkelling and having fun.

I knew what I was doing with tools, the farming life had made sure I could fix a broken thing or start a stopped thing, and as the rainy days were fewer and further between I found my place just offshore, with the two of them, helping with the manual labour.

In the beginning we were making benches and acid scrubbing the rust from around the hull, but it was easy enough with some music and a beer at the end of the day. Eventually we would get to the 'pimping it up' part, hanging hammocks, wiring the music system and building a small bar out of ice boxes.

The most important fixture on this ship was a part of the engine, it was a multi-use piece of equipment that when dropped into the engine room would swear, fight, plead and finally come up covered in grease with a smile on its face – this was, of course, Dennis.

'Come on you bloody bitch you!' came from below, clanking and splashing, an almost black hand came out of the hatch 'a ratchet Clem me lad'. Six more minutes of sexual profanities towards his tools and the engine itself and Dennis popped up and out like a 63 year old shouldn't be able to. 'Let's give her a go shall we?'

The engine shook like an addict and coughed to life. 'Yes my boy! We bloody done it!' Dennis already had his hand in the beer cooler.

'You know what time it is?'

'Beer o'clock?'

'Tomorrow we are good to go, my boy, let's get into the bars and find some sexy people to get on this party platform.'

'Where are they going with all this?'

'Going?'

'What are they doing? As in, what is the aim?'

'Oh!' It was a good question, I had thought about it but hadn't answered myself. However I was close to a conclusion to a different question I had asked myself earlier and I had a sneaky suspicion that the answer was that Lemon was indeed smart. This made it difficult to give answers to things I didn't know much about in the hope that she wouldn't notice. 'I guess they are trying to take over ...'

'Take over the world?' she blinked, this slow-blink I had become accustomed to as a tick when she was removing the emotion from a statement. I was a little suspicious that this was a sneaky way of hearing my uninfluenced opinion before she revealed hers; the blink would cover a smile or a stare, or a look of contentment, or a flash of disgust in her eyes.

I tried to work around this, 'They are spreading over the space.' Why was I pretending I understood, when I clearly didn't?

'There has to be a reason, don't you think, to just keep taking over?'

The last few hours had unfurled an interlocked stone road down the island's main street and pushed a grid-like hotel into the space that was once huts made from trees and dry grass. The speed that time passed on the orb meant that their season had come and gone in those two hours, and although the people on the island had covered the sand with a layer of stone, other countries were working much faster. An asphalt scar had split through the desert in Dubai and minutes later the first death caused a traffic jam, filling this highway with standing cars. Lemon had been watching Jakarta spread like blood on tissue paper, and mere minutes with my eyes away from the island showed me Tel Aviv splintering up the West coast of Israel like salt crystals forming on a string. It was anxiety inducing and the question 'where are they going with all this?' might be the ultimate one.

Through my ignorance I had a theory, I tried it out on Lemon; 'They are driven by three things, the people.'

'Okay,' she raised an eyebrow, knowing I was already unsure of myself, the blink didn't even hide the glint of 'impress me'.

'Well, there are three different type of people, who are driven by a separate thing each,' I back-pedalled as my first point disproved itself before it left my mouth.

'Sure,' she held a straight face, it was kind of her to give me that moment to collect my thoughts.

'The people who like the people; the people who care about how other people see them, and the people who are scared of what might happen,' errgh, okay that came out a little on the weak side.

Lemon didn't speak, she just bounced her hair from side to side in an arc, I had no idea what it meant ...

'The people who like the people are often trying to find a way to help other people as well as themselves,' I started, 'they are happy if they can make other people happy,' I continued.

'Surely that fits them into the second group?'

'Umm, wait,'

'I don't know, sorry continue.'

I wasn't sure I wanted to now, but here goes, 'Most of the people care about how others see them, but it makes no sense to build seventy hotels and save a million dollars if they can live in one house with two meals each day, the only reason they would do so much more is so that other people can see them doing it.'

'Okay, true,' Lemon agreed, and added, 'but those people like it when others see them as the one who is building all the hotels?'

'I don't know if it's like that,' I tried.

'It's like an addiction?' she offered.

Somehow that made sense, but I wasn't sure how.

Chapter 38 – think on your feet

I woke up with a pocket full of Thai Baht, more money than I've had in a long time. It wasn't mine but it had been a successful night, I had taken a deposit from, and hand written individual boat tickets for, almost thirty people who would be joining us on the boat today. Badly scribbled maps for where to meet and promises of what the day would be like became harder to read and more inflated as the night grew late.

Dennis was waiting with a beer and a - 'So what's it looking like lad?' and, 'A lot of lovely ladies coming along I hope?'

I wished I could remember who was coming, but two hours of scrabbling around and trying to get everything ready filled the time right up until our first guests arrived – and they were everything that Dennis had hoped for! Not a cloud, drinks on ice, chilled out music and cliff jumping ... wait, cliff jumping?

Nate stayed at the bottom of the cliff, helping the people in and out of the boat. Dennis had a full time job of keeping it close to the cliff without swiping the trees with the mast.

I climbed the rocky passage that I had never been up, to a spot where I had never stood, and then there I was at the top of a cliff, telling people to jump off.

'Is it completely safe?'

'People jump here a lot.'

'When do I jump?'

'Now.'

'Do people ever hurt themselves?'

'People jump here a lot.'

Finally the last person who wanted to jump, had jumped, success!

Now I had to throw myself off the cliff to catch up with the circling boat. Whoa! That's high! How did all these people jump off so easily? Oh well, no time to think.

If you've never tried cliff jumping, it's like this: You are scared at the top, then you jump off and it's scary, everything is whooshing and then you're really deep under water. It's a strange thing to do with your time.

The net that dragged by the side of the boat was christened 'The Sea Jacuzzi', just like cliff jumping, I had never tried it before, but today was going to be a day of firsts.

Nate was explaining the entrance and exit technique to the group when he added, 'So if you all watch Clem, he's going to demonstrate how to jump into the net safely.'

I am? Oh, 'I am!' – 'What do I do?'

'Jump into the net.'

'Oh, okay,' and that was that.

If you've never tried a 'Sea Jacuzzi' before, your first time might be a little like this: Much like cliff jumping, you jump into the water and everything moves really fast. Unlike cliff jumping you try to grab onto a net, get your foot caught, struggle under the water, untangle a bit, drag yourself up the net and realise your swimming shorts are mostly by your knees. You can try and pull them up but if you lose your grip you will find yourself somewhere in the sea, not being a very good demonstrator.

The rest of the trip was quite the same. Things fell in the sea, people fell after them. We ate rice, of course, and stayed between the islands for the sunset. All in all everyone ended up drunk, bruised, exhausted and happy by the time we touched the pier - then came the after party.

'And the third group?'

'The people who are scared of what might happen,' I stalled, repeating myself.

'The ones who guessed right?' She was correct, but I was hoping it wasn't that simple. 'They are the most interesting I think.'

I agreed and added, 'They are doing the things they do, not because they want to, or because they like it, but because they don't know what will happen if they don't.'

'What do they think will happen?' she asked.

Again I had a feeling she knew the path of the conversation already. 'They think that if they are good people, good things will happen to them.'

'Oh, like karma?'

'Not karma, I'm talking about the people who think there is more outside their world'

'So they are good, because they think that there is more to life than living and dying?' she gave a tiny shake of her head, 'the people who think they go to another place after they die, right? The pond people!' It still wasn't that funny. I laughed at it again.

Lemon raised a finger as she ran through a thought process, it hovered as she said, 'So if they are good, then they go to this place after they die?' it sounded like a question but the finger didn't move, 'but if they are bad, they stay here?'

'Oh, no, there's like another place, but not a good place,' I wasn't sure about this part, they talked a lot about the other place but this one was a bit more open to interpretation.

'So if they are good then good things happen,' she put that finger up again, 'and if they are bad, bad things happen,' it still stood there, for some reason it kept me silent, she finalised the thought, 'just like karma!'

'I guess so,' I tried, it was a good point, 'but karma is like, when they think that good things they do will be returned to them later on, but just later on that year or something.'

'Sounds made up,' she said, bluntly.

Why do I feel like I'm defending karma now? Both concepts were a bit shaky.

'So these people are the people who are afraid of what might happen?'

Was it a question? It sounded like a question and the finger wasn't hovering.

Okay, I guess it was a question, 'Yes?'

'They fit into the second group, the people who ...'

'No!' no raised finger meant I could interrupt anytime, 'they do things so they will get a better,' wait, now I didn't know! '... at the end ... and so ...'

'So they are the people who do things because they care what others think. Also!'

'It's not quite that black and white,' I tried.

'It's about as black and white as grouping all the people into three,' she tilted her head at me.

In the time we spoke, the island dipped to night and back. Maybe it should be 'everybody does things for a reason' and not 'everything happens for a reason'. It fits so well in a dark untrusting way. We were no closer to answering 'where are they going with all this?' when the first of the boats split from the island. Then it looked like a packet of seeds spilling out of the harbour, at least twice as many as there were a few hours ago.

Chapter 39 – fast-forward

Throughout the day I took a few hundred photos on the boat's shockproof-waterproof camera – people cliff jumping, diving board flips, in the sea Jacuzzi, underwater shots and the never-ending Thai sunset.

This was how we sold the next day's tickets, scrolling the photos across the big screen at the after-party made the job easy, people would just ask how they could also go out on what looked like an epic day – and we would tell them 'get your ticket for tomorrow, if you're ready for it'.

I set up a little green initiative on our trips - cleaning up paradise! Every time we crossed over to the monkey beach, where the most trash would be found, we would take some garbage bags and as we started collecting rubbish - so would the customers. We could pick up several bags of plastic waste each day.

The litter wasn't just the tourists' fault, a lot was washed up, but the monkeys' skilful criminal capabilities added to it. They lured people closer and closer by looking cute, right up until when they jumped on their packs and, within minutes, pulled out their belongings, scattering them around on the beach, mostly looking for food but partly just in the name of mischief.

It was undoubtedly the best summer I had ever had in my life! Each day on the boat was one and the same party. We went out most days, swimming, jumping, drinking and partying with groups from all over the world - with the after-party video easily filling the next day's boat. We were living the dream – until it happened.

It was a complete engine seizure, the boat ground to a halt on the return straight of another incredible day. It could have been worse, we were already entering the harbour and with a little help we managed to tie the boat to a buoy line and taxi-boat the guests to shore.

It was to be the last after-party of the summer for, even with Dennis managing to temporarily fix the problem, the boat had to leave the island and get to a bigger port where it could be fixed properly, a job that would easily take most of the rest of the high season.

With it went my job and my bed.

Chapter 40 – step nine

This time I had no shoes, but my feet were hard from the ground grinding on them every day, the air was cool and damp with the changing season. The jungle didn't skip and play today as I trod a well walked path into the thick green and turned onto the sparse path that I knew well from my jungle runs – the truth was that the boat leaving had given me the opportunity to do what I had thought about every day from day one on the island.

The summer had been a non-stop high, but I had strayed far from the reason I found myself here in the first place. I needed my feet to be bare, I needed to be penniless. I came here to discover, explore, survive and find out what I really needed to be happy in this world – to do this, I would need to start at the bottom, and of course, I planned on eating coconuts.

So, fighting the over-westernised brain I had redeveloped though Boon's tattoo shop and from selling boat tickets, I reset completely.

I found a perfect sleeping spot, completely walled off by trees from any hikers who made it far enough, and on the other side just a spectacular drop to the next plateau. The sunset cut across the mouth of the opening and lit up the entire town from where I slept, that amazing orange glow from the low Thai sun was worth the bug bites. This wasn't being poor anymore, this was breathing free. An hour scramble would take me down to the throngs of tourists and an hour back would be my nirvana.

Many days I didn't want to leave at all, but the jungle didn't provide everything I needed so I would climb down, strip and wash in the same spot below the ledge then double back, across the foot of the cliff and down to sea level at the one end of the beach, walking into the sun as if I were a flashpacker who'd just left their hotel for a morning swim. Tanned, fit, strong and salty wasn't a bad look and definitely helped me get some work; it was liberating, sleeping where I liked, knowing that rent wasn't due and the rice bag with all my possessions was always stowed away on the hill. If you worked you were paid, if you didn't - then you weren't and you had to find another option, there was no 'must' in my life.

The tattoo shop I had built up from scratch, after all that time spent keeping it white and clean and friendly and fun, now looked like all the others, truly Thai crack-denned dirty - and empty. It was a shame to see, but a little bit of satisfaction that Boon wasn't riding on my work after he lied so much.

I avoided rainy nights by staying late in whichever bar was open, it wasn't too bad but I knew that the bugs and the dew would get me in the end so I decided to use what I had to make a shelter - and now, I will share this with you:

How to make a jungle house out of clear food wrap!
What you'll need: 1 x knife or sharp blade. 1x catering size roll of plastic wrap, anything up to 150 meters will do. 20 minutes construction time. No shame.
Step one: find three or four trees, preferably in the shade and with two of them spaced at least six foot away from each other.
Step two: clean the area between them; all the rocks and sticks need to go.

Step three: take the cling wrap and start at the bottom of one trunk, a few turns to secure the end.

Step four: walk around the three or four trees wrapping them in plastic wrap, working upwards overlapping each layer until you reach head height, leaving one corner a single turn higher than the others.

Step five: make a few turns around one trunk to secure the change of direction, then by sliding under the walls and reaching over the top, wrap the walls together by going up the outside of one wall, across the open 'roof', down the outside of the other wall and around across the ground. Start on the lowest corner so the overlap climbs and liquid would run from layer to layer and off the roof.

Step six: it gets more difficult but try to reach between the roof layers to wrap the entire structure one more time in the final direction starting again at the lowest point, so all four walls have overlapping wrap going horizontally and vertically, sealing off the space inside completely.

Step seven: take a few lengths of wrap and press them down the centre of one wall, making the area thicker, and with a sharp blade and cut down the centre of this thick area keeping inside the patch. This will be your door.

Step eight: the final step is to step inside, turn around and press a few lengths of wrap over the opening you just entered by, sealing yourself inside and the mosquitoes out.

Step nine: lie on the floor.

The longer you want to stay there the more wrap you can apply, just be sure to layer it from the lowest point to the highest point so that liquid travels down the wrap, running from one layer to part way down the next, not wrapping it from top to bottom so water runs between the folds.

You shouldn't suffocate in here, shouldn't. I recommend laying on some clothes or a sheet to keep from sticking to the plastic floor and making it before sunset so you don't trap any mosquitoes inside with you.

This is where I slept, mostly comfy and basically bug free.

Sometimes it's hard to tell if I chose this option because it was the best choice at the time, or just because I wanted to live out the Jungle Book dream of climbing a palm to cut down fresh coconuts, but couldn't quite hack sleeping in a tree. The coconuts were my backup plan and now my Baht had all been spent, I had to get active on my first harvest.

There was a place I had explored before where there were coconuts just laying around where they had fallen - at least that's what I remembered. In reality there was not a floor coconut in sight. Not many in the sky either, a few clustered on giant looping palms, dark and hidden amongst the abundance of leaves. I would have to climb up and get one, it should be fine.

It wasn't fine.

Imagine a boy, his feet only forty centimetres above the ground, feet dug into the sharp husky trunk of a very tall tree. Legs bent so much that if they were straight he would be standing on the ground, both hands kind-of clamping the same smooth piece of bark. Just hovering there, not willing to push up because it would hurt too much, not willing to step down because of stubbornness. Just hovering there.

All alone in a jungle which had been getting darker this whole time. Far from my greatest moment, I let it drag out way too long before I lost strength and stepped down. I don't know, I just figured I would be able to climb the tree, but instead I sat on the floor, which is not nearly as impressive.

The town was close, and nothing was stopping me going back. If I asked for some help or some food I would probably get it, maybe it was learning that I can't climb a coconut tree or maybe it was my need to feel self-reliant and free - but I decided to stick with the coconut farming idea.

I found a much shorter tree that seemed a little less intimidating, and made my master-plan. Looping the neck and hem of the final t-shirt around my feet I made it curve around the trunk so it sat over the rough husks, palms still flat on the sides of the husks I wiggled my way up. A few meters above the ground I was already feeling victorious, the t-shirt was hooked on the upward bladed edges of the bark and I was ... *rrriiip* ... the t-shirt tore open where it held my weight and I dropped - my mistake was trying to grab onto the trunk as I fell. So there I sat, in the dirt, my arms and legs raw and sore from scraping down the entire height I had climbed.

My bohemian safety net had holes big enough to fall through – I had to accept that I absolutely could not survive on coconuts, because I couldn't pick coconuts. Not a single one.

She inhaled, about to speak. Waited a few more seconds and said, 'I like the silence.'
'Me too,' I just told the truth but did Lemon just lie to me? She hates the silence, this I knew.
'It's good to think sometimes.'
The small white lie landed easy, I didn't mind. I was intrigued, why would this cool, confident person to my left need to present herself any different than who she already is. 'What do you think about?' I filled the gap in the conversation.
'Things and stuff, ya know.'
I didn't know. Things and stuff? Lemon was great, smart, kind but she rarely let a second pass without starting a new topic, I was pretty sure she mostly thought about filling the silence. Sometimes I lied to her, of course, to make myself look better. She wouldn't feel the need to do that would she? Not to me. That was a long pause, I was missing my turn in the talk, 'What stuff?' I asked, anticlimactically as per usual.

'The people, in your, your thing ...' she gestured towards the globe, 'they have these ideas, about why they are here.'
I waited; maybe I was a judgemental ass.
'Did you ever think, that it's maybe possible, that someone somewhere is looking down at us thinking, when will they kiss?'
Freeze frame, sweat prickles, welling eyes. I swallowed an imaginary apple. She leant close to me all in one bob of a movement, pecked my cheek once with a

small soft suction release noise, and bobbed back. A river was running down my chest. I said something like 'hur'

'I would tell them, soon, if they asked.'

My ears popped, her scent lingered from her swoop-in, why was my mouth so dry? 'Okay.'

'Okay!' she said, 'now, what's new down here?' she turned back to the orb, which I had been staring intently into for this entire ordeal, and relieving the tension she asked, 'I wonder how Aiko and Akari are doing?'

I tried to breathe normally.

Chapter 41 – sex pizza

It was the end of August and on my way home it flecked with rain a little ...

The rock climbing community would call it 'Dirtbagging', a state of comfort or desperation when one eats the leftovers from literally anywhere. I had semi-perfected the skill of passing through a restaurant just before a table was going to be cleared, and clearing anything that looked edible on my way past. Ideally I would aim for something easy to pick up in motion – pizzas, garlic bread, a slice of cake – anything that hadn't been played with or spread around the place, singular pieces were my bread and butter.

Knocking it up a notch was the crème de la crème of dirtbag-life, the fake waiter 'are you guys all done with this?' move. Aided by the huge rip in my only t-shirt being mostly in the back, and targeting mostly couples who were usually less disgusting and more distracted, it turned out that once the half-finished plate had been pushed to one side you can simply walked over with a 'are you guys all done with this?' and a 'no problem, I'll clear that away for you' and relocate the plate to another table where you could sit down to enjoy your meal.

The third notch, maybe the most fun, but not the most honourable, was what I liked to call 'sex pizza' – although it covered all foods and drinks, it is exactly what you imagine. Hopefully.

The premise was simple – be honest.
'So did you want to get something to eat later?' she

says.

'Actually I'm kind of dirtbagging it right now, so I should avoid legitimate establishments.'

'Dirtbagging it?'

'Oh, just eating leftovers from restaurants and cafés when someone doesn't finished their plate.'

'Oh no! You can't do that!'

'It's good for the environment.'

'Let's get something to eat, I'm paying.'

'Well, if you insist!'

Anyway, as I was saying, it flecked with rain a little. A few drips at three o'clock in the morning whilst walking under the bright moon showing itself between heavy clouds. The contrast threw off my night vision and the light patches were shorter each time, I was already along the well-trodden path when the splatters turned into rain, but by the time I was at the base of the scramble, the rain was drumming down hard through the jungle canopy.

It took seconds for the stony earth slope to be sealed off by a sheet of water, parting at my ankles and spraying into my face when I reached for a tree root ahead of me. I might have been okay if it weren't for the 'bits' – bits came down from a jungle that hadn't been washed through for a month, bits of sticks, bits of stone, a snake. 'Whoa..!' I snatched my hand back from where the dark winding object slid over the edge of the next ledge. I don't think it was a snake, the way it didn't bend but bounced past me, but it definitely got me thinking about what might actually be washing down this path.

By now I was pretty keen on turning back to the bar, but that rice bag up there had all my savings in it, even if it was only just over 500 baht.

My 'house' was almost intact, well the top section. Rain drummed into the cling-film roof bouncing together and running down the lower edge. The rain water had found its way through the trees and made paths to wash the debris along with it, one of these paths had found its way right through the side of my little home where the plastic wrap had been no match for the sticks and roots that came down the stream. Already brown water welled around inside the ground-sheet finding ways to escape through the wall on the other side.

I dug my rice bag out of its hiding place, where it was getting close to submersion then, throwing it down the slope onto a ledge that wasn't already a river, I climbed back down, snatched it up and made my way back to the beach.

Chapter 42 – choices

Coconuts and cling film had already caused enough problems so following the advice of a local I went to the most run-down side of town. Leaving my rice bag hidden outside, and trying to look reliable, I went to find somewhere that I could afford to sleep in – I thought broken beds and missing doors were the best I was going to get but I found a room at the top floor of a guesthouse that must have been made from the accidental leftover space when the other rooms were built. It was closer to the centre than I thought I would be able to afford and even though the walls were only plasterboard reaching a foot shy of the roof, it had its own charm, and a working door - which is always a plus.

The bed was a foam mattress on the floor and the fan had a personality of its own; summoning enough shaking momentum to find itself in a completely different place in the morning than it was the night before and just gently blowing air towards the wall. Best of all if you pushed the right place on the outside of the wall a broken panel folded in and you could reach around and unlock the door from inside if you were locked out. It was perfect, the price was right and I wouldn't have to worry about losing my key.

Through time I readjusted to an actual 'room' and, with the few tourists who made it through the monsoon, I had reached somewhere just above 'simply surviving – shelter water and food' - things were looking up!

Most nights I would end up at the island's High Bar, a 24 hour spot just inside the jungle's edge where they sold marijuana as well as alcohol. I'm not a big fan of smoking weed but the people it draws in are a good sort and nobody asks too many questions when they are floating backwards through their seat.

It was a small area, just a wooden kiosk style counter with a straw roof. The main area had a barbeque with a few tables and chairs but most people sat on these wooden platforms raised on bamboo stumps that stood at different levels down the rocks towards the cliff edge.

Behind the bar were two battered bamboo shacks like the one I used to live in, mostly hidden by the overgrowth which broke through the walls in some places. Actually most of the bar was like this too and trees, growing through the floors and between the platforms, had been wrapped with fairy lights to show people the way through the multi-level smoking area.

After a while coming and going each night I got to know the guys who ran the bar, all young travellers who had fallen on their feet and found a place where police could be bribed. They told me that if I needed some work in exchange for drinks I should ask them; mostly I would be lighting a nightly BBQ and doing a bit of bartending.

Chapter 43 – mosquito borne

I felt weak. I woke early with the intention of ending the day with a job that paid real money, but part way down Beach road I felt myself struggling to hold myself steady.

Walking slow and keeping to the side of the road to let people pass, I had to steady my breath just to control these waves of weakness followed by nausea. I would be fine if I could just lie down in the dark of my room a little longer, so I turned my back to the beach and it was a blur - my vision caught up a second later - it took just two more steps before my insides shot up into my throat.

My instant reaction was to try and block the explosion. My hand hit my mouth, palm flat with a clap and the contents of my stomach hit it with full force. Lurching forward with my hand over my mouth, what seemed like a pint of hot vomit filled the gap between lips and palm and took the only way out. The escape route was between my thumb and wrist which had left a small space to perfectly redirect the puke in what could only be described as a spectacularly targeted slightly downward angled spray to the side, it was white and curdled and it hit a small Chinese boy in the face.

It was a split second, just a 'ffttt' but so much liquid. I remember it in slow motion, one moment the family of four were walking by. The boy maybe five, wearing glasses and crocs, little yellow ducks on his white t-shirt - nanoseconds later his entire face was hit with force by enough upchuck to mask him completely – I glanced just to register the scene, the smell that was from the seventh circle of hell itself, the child now dripping chunks from his little spectacles letting out a wail like an air raid siren. It was over. I've never seen a man look so scared and affronted as the father, I put one hand out and heaved past them all.

Filling the space between two plant pots and painting the grill of an open drain I splashed my way to safety. Tik tik, hurgh, tik. I'm suddenly cold? I feel like my blood is barely moving, what's that noise even? TIK!

Splat, a wet foot hit the floor inside my door, turning to shut it behind me started the spinning. Wheeeee this whining noise in my ears – I'm not in a good way. Staring around the cracked side of the mirror, whoa that's some black bags. I had to sit down - what's wrong with me?

I had a feeling I was in for a rough night and vowed to re-start the job search in the morning - what followed was an eight day sweat-lodge session of malnutrition, dehydration and mosquito-borne Dengue Fever. If you've never had it - I don't recommend it.

Healthcare would have been great but as that was out of the question I bought a ticket to the 'sweat-it-out' show. I would be in the poor-man's medical limbo within hours, I prepared for something I knew nothing about; water, lots of it, five litre bottles to each side and an empty in the middle, deep breaths. The bed was like a hot plate and my clothes became suffocating, I managed to lock the door and shutters to turn the room into a box, I wasn't sure what was coming but uninsured, broke and close to collapse already, I waited. It began.

Fever spiked with headaches like I never knew could be had, everything itched, I sat naked on the floor sweat pooling off my back and balls. Taking a sip every ten seconds, the water tasted different each time, arms shaking just bringing the bottle up to my lips.

Time slowed and sped at will, confusion was the torment, I kept forgetting what I was doing. Audio hallucinations amplified noises from the street. I think my nose is bleeding. Day two, maybe, I don't know. I was weak, really weak. Sip, sip - still no pee.

Everything itches so much. My eyeballs feel sharp, I caught myself laying my face on the floor and tipping the bottle to my face, it was hard to drink any more but I was endlessly thirsty.

The crack under the door dipped to black and back, I don't know if I slept. My bones felt too big for my skin, the ache was ceaseless. Finally, on my hands and knees, hanging into an empty bottle, my urine came out dark, smelling like cheap soap. My mouth filled with saliva every second, sip, spit. Repeat.

Knocking on the door; so loud! The door handle rattling in my head, then more knocking – I stayed silent, if the door opened the scene would have been a rough one. Thai voices and nothing – I hadn't paid rent in days, did I even have enough? I can't think about that now, I'm too busy trying not to puke.

Lifting myself up from body-hot tiles to shift to a cooler section, I reposition myself around the room in the dark, a map of warm wet outlines in my wake.

On my knees, over a half full bottle of pee 'hi Clem' 'hi Clem' 'how are you Clem?' 'not good Clem' my mind went to stranger places.

Have you ever tried to vomit into a bottle? It goes wrong. Into a bottle half full with pee? Air is displaced with liquid and that air smells bad – reaction, more vomit, all water.

Pass out. It could have been days for all I could sense.

Come to, with some air in my lungs, everything hurt but the crippling feeling of debilitation had subsided. I sat up for a while before trying to stand, then pulling the shorts on I screwed up my eyes for the outside, it wasn't so bad after all.

Chapter 44 – heading to high ground

Each milestone gives you a new philosophy, potential and realisation.

I reject those who claim delusion is a state of mind symptomatic of a mental disorder, from where I am standing at least. Maybe I would venture so far as to claim it was a reaction to denial and stubbornness, in a bid for freedom, however you perceive it – reality is the roadblock.

We sat in the High Bar, watching the sea. Behind me was one of the bamboo huts, my bamboo hut, offered to me as long as I stayed. The dengue fever had used up the last few days safety net of rent that I needed to save enough money to pay for another week in the room. It had only been two weeks since I had gathered the tatters of plastic wrap pooling around the four trees - it hadn't rained since.

So the High Bar, what did we do up here? We ignored reality.

More than the tourists who visit the island? No, not if they weren't blind. Not more than any traveller to Asia with a sense of this world. The difference? We had to ignore it for longer, the constant belief that something in front of your eyes just isn't there, that resulted in delusion.

There were four of us. I won't be going back, so in my bid to protect the identities of western drug dealers in Thailand, I'll be avoiding names and simply using a 'He' and 'She' system. First things first, we all thought we were doing something impressive.

Things you need to know as a Westerner in Thailand:

You don't own it, whatever it is. If you think you own it, you're being set up.

'Who's bar is it?'

'It's our bar.'

This is a mistake! Are you Thai? No? Then it's not yours. Even if you are Thai it's probably not yours.

Island politics are dangerous. I had previous experience, of course, when it came to the money versus life skew. You better believe you are worth less than the land you stand on. In a sick way, the closer you are to the jungle, the less you're worth, you could be gone in ten minutes and snake shit in a few weeks.

The police work for money, not morals. Don't think the handshake and the 16,000 baht mean you have a deal.

Paying a bribe and saying, 'we have police protection' is a mistake. You do not! You have police ignorance. The vast plain between ignoring and protecting is flecked with the blood of Westerners who filled in the gap themselves.

The mafia still own the land. Call them what you like, thugs, families, gangs – the Thai version of the Mafia are all these things. Maybe not as organised but definitely as brutal, the pyramid is the same and the dirt you stand on belongs to someone – and that someone has the last word.

'I know the big boss,' is a mistake. You know nobody, you know a manager of a branch, a man capable of dirty work. The big boss doesn't talk to you, he doesn't care who you are and he wouldn't know if you died today. We hang off the lowest rung of this society, with the meth-heads and the thieves - people with no leverage all out for themselves.

The danger is being amongst those who also merely want to survive.

'We are the gods upon Olympia' actually left someone's lips up there on that ledge. I looked over to the dark mountain across the bay, its daily loom spread our way soon after the sunset, its shadow close to the foot of our cliff.

'Maybe *that* is Olympia, we are more dogs than gods' my brain looped through thoughts that rarely finished before the next interrupted - I still held some stock in reality since the last time I had believed I was ahead, and the time before, if I really put my mind to it I could still taste that stinking blade.

They were nice guys, really easy going. It wasn't my place to preach, and it was impressive to set up the space, find the right corrupt policeman, import marijuana in bulk and have made it this far without getting strung up in the jungle. So maybe the guy behind it did have some leverage – I packed weed into a shisha for some Spanish backpackers, and climbed back into my hammock.

Chapter 45 – thieves in the night

We didn't leave the bar, almost ever. It was a 24 hour bar behind which we spent, drank, smoked and fucked. Trips into the town were like walking into the sun after weeks underground, the noise and lights were so far from our mind-set – we went only for supplies.

It would be safe to say I fell right back into it, the Island Eyes. The ignorance of consequence and reality became the silk sheets between my skin and bones and the bug ridden bamboo floor. This bubble was inside the bubble – intensifying delusion and hedonism - it gave us ridiculous priorities.

I didn't really *do* anything, and I didn't know how the bar made money. The monthly 'rent' went somewhere so somewhere it must have come from, savings from before maybe? 'Wake and bake' was a daily ritual for everyone but myself, I preferred rum for breakfast as the others plumed smoke. We carved our names into the woodwork with the tip of a machete, teaching ourselves to spin fire and convincing each other that we were capable of things which we would never follow through.

The problem with delusion is that when, by chance, it's backed up by and masked as reality, you become fully invested. In reality actions have consequences, so when they don't you make up your own reasons why.

First it was the thief. I knew him from before, he used to work for my old friend Gan. This guy was strung out, skinny and way down the meth rabbit hole – by now I knew the signs. I'll write this with as much drama as I felt in the moment when someone caught him with his hand over the bar in the money box. We chased him with knives.

It was no more than that. It shouldn't be easy to draw a machete on another human, maybe we didn't consider what we would do if we caught him – the concern was the lack of adrenaline, the way the act sat on the same emotional level as pouring a drink.

Life reached a cacophony of unreal. A blur of fire, flesh and poultry.

'Do you think you're the only one?'

'Only one to make a world?'

'No, not the world part, the people part. Do you think anyone else has made people who, you know - live?'

'It's possible someone has made something just like this, but it's not likely that they are very much the same,' I thought about the failed attempts that didn't survive.

She read my mind, 'Are these the first people, or did you try some other designs first?'

'They're not the first, but they made sure that they survived, well it was half them and half luck.'

Lemon paused a second before asking, 'Because you made them more intelligent than the other animals?'

'No, not that,' I assured, 'they survived because of their hands, they can hold things.'

'Yes, so can chameleons.'

'Yes, but they are smarter than the chameleons,' this was true. 'Chameleons are stupid.'

'But very beautiful.'

'Yes,' we were getting off topic, 'and small.'

'So if chameleons were really big, they would be control the world instead?'

I thought for a moment, yes, I'll go down this road, 'Tried that - didn't work.'

'What happened?' she asked, perking up again.

'What a mess,' I told her, 'the lizard creatures could only adapt by getting bigger or smaller, they went with bigger, growing bigger and bigger until they were too big to survive any changes - and this world always changes.'

'And so they just died out.'

'Exactly!' I smiled at her, 'it took a long time before I could make animals that could adapt in other ways as the world changed.'

'What did the people think of the giant lizards?' she asked.

'They never met them - they came long time after,' I told her, 'but when they find the remains of one they get very excited.'

'What do you mean by 'came along'?' Lemon asked, 'Do you mean you didn't make them like they are now?'

Chapter 46 – chickens and near misses

This was the beginning of a chapter of my life that I refer to as 'pushing my luck' – and as all epic tales of delusion begin, poultry took centre stage.

So I bought two chickens, it was on a whim I guess. They were just there, scratching around in the dirt - they did look a little sad. They weren't for sale but if you don't ask you never know – these two scrawny-ass moulting black birds were gratefully swapped for 200 baht each and joined me on my lazy wander back to the bar.

I upended a few unused tables and put them side by side behind the bar, wrapping a torn fishing net around the legs and stretching it over the top, this would of course be the chickens own personal area where they would have to stay at night, what with the stray cats that would come scouting for scraps.

Growing up on a farm you learn quickly that naming animals isn't always a good idea, but I wasn't one to take advice so I went ahead and named the quietest chicken Emily. Her companion, Shafique Muhammed Ibbun Kahn, was the more adventurous of the pair, orchestrating some form of prison-break each and every night.

So the scene has been set; two chickens, each with their own merit – each one with their own unique destiny.

'Sam, song, nung,' I counted down in Thai, as my co-worker put the home-made cardboard dinosaur head over his own. I stabbed it in the face with a long knife, then four times in the top, and finally one more right in the front.

A girl screamed with laughter that quickly turned to, 'Stop!'

'I saw that!' He pulled the box off his head, 'Right there!' He indicated an inch between two fingers, this was how far the knife went from his face. 'Okay fuck this,' he said, putting the box over my head.

'Don't stab me in the face man, don't stab me in the face,' I said.

Someone in the background spoke shrilly, 'Careful guys!' The camera shook out of scene and back onto the weapon wielder.

'Hi' he said again, followed by inaudible muttering and one huge hack with the knife right through the front of the dinosaurs face, pulling it right off my head.

'That was right next to my face!' I said, reeling back – followed by more inaudible ruckus and myself throwing the split open cardboard head towards the camera.

'Whoa! When was this?' We had watched the video maybe ten times; it was slightly disconcerting that nobody remembered any of it happening. We had felt our faces the first time we watched - they were still in one piece. The fancy dress dino-face was hacked to pieces and half the rum was gone. Normally putting a knife through a box inches from your friend's face would affect you, make you slow down. The thought that 'we were actually indestructible' was the problem here.

You see the pattern; to fully immerse yourself in a delusion you need luck. Just three or four things that don't come back to bite you - and you can offset any reality checks as anomalies.

It was as if we were racing to get some sort of comeuppance.

Chapter 47 - longtails

People often say 'yes, it's amazing, but you're living in a bubble' – I don't see why this is a bad thing. Inside the island bubble and outside, it's just life. One is better than the other. Why do people reject a life they would thoroughly enjoy simply because it's different, and therefore a bubble?

They would argue, as they often do, that it's disconnected from the outside world, and that you don't know what's going on everywhere else. Good! People weren't happier before they knew too much, I guess, but they must have had less long-term anxiety, and maybe a higher general self-esteem. Anyway, I'm getting off track, inside the bubble and outside the bubble; they are both still very firmly in reality. Right now, I was in a bubble, in a bubble.

It was a plan to have more fun, to do something that was mine again, to burst my little bubble. Hypocritical? Yes! But this bubble was in danger of becoming a mental one and not merely a physical area – I hadn't jumped off a cliff, or pushed a boat out, or chased a monkey in months and the need for adventure was on my mind.

The opportunity came to me, prompted by the high season ending earlier than usual - the wooden Thai-style long tail boat drivers had to find another way to get tourists out on the water. In the summer all they had to do was stand around the pier asking 'want taxi boat, mai?' – there were always enough people wanting to go somewhere.

'Mr Kim!' I was trying to keep fit and take a break from the knife play, running the beaches instead of the jungle because when the rain came, the steep paths where I used to run became slippery mud troughs. 'Kim, what you do?'

It was Sid, a longtail boat captain who had once ferried our customers to Dennis' boat when the water was too rough to get close enough to land.

'I'm in the high ... I work in a bar,' I told him.

'Have customer, mai?' Sid questioned me, 'Need longtail?'

'Have customer sometime,' I told the truth, the bar was quiet but we would often get group of travellers who had clustered together en-route to combat the uncomfortableness of quiet bars and empty dorms.

'Them need longtail, mai?' Sid asked again, he was young for a captain, and easy going compared to many of them. 'If need, talk Sid, okay?'

The weather was on and off with the season change, one day would be warm, calm and sunny – the next a relentless downpour reshaping the islands outline. It was hard to predict more than a day in the future so pre-booking boat trips had become difficult.

Back in the High Bar, coincidentally, we had one of these groups - mostly American, some Canadian and a few Swedes – there to smoke in the sunset. As usual they'd asked what they could do on the island, an idea clicked into place.

There was a lagoon, a beautiful shallow blue cookie cut-out of the cliff face, on one of the uninhabited islands not far from here, I knew it was the perfect spot - the next day should be sunny but still a little windy so this sea-lagoon inside the high cliffs would be one of the best places to swim and stay warm.

'How long will you be here?' I asked.

'All night,' was the general consensus of the group, I ran to find Sid again.

This was the first of my trips, taking eight of them to the lagoon in Sid's boat, Thai style BBQ in the lagoon, an ice box and telling them to bring their own drinks. Sid played guitar on the nose of the longtail, I just had fun. On our way out of the lagoon I took them to the same cliff jumping spot Dennis had taken me, and we stopped between the islands for the sunset before going back to the High Bar for an after party.

Chapter 48 – the bitey end

Thai people can't hurt snakes, here's why; snakes are, on the whole, the protectors of the land. It's not 100% religious, although that's what's been claimed by most of my friends, but in general it's good old superstition – one guy said it was a bad idea to kill snakes so everyone else was like 'okay' and from this point on they had to find someone else to kill snakes for them.

I like snakes. They are creepy and reptilian as a true realisation and reminder that if I were born 60,000 years ago I could have been embryo soup. Nonetheless snakes are impressive, but some of the monsters that had made their way down here and out of the jungle were a little more than impressive.

Tiny cat was super cute. Sometimes when I was drunk enough I would put her head in my mouth, she really didn't mind. This little kitten ran around the bar abusing my chickens and causing all sorts of feline related problems. Lucy was also cute, not a cat I knew well but she meant a lot to the girl who worked with us, she fed her every morning outside our bungalow. The other cat was a cat, I don't remember its name but it was around and about, maybe it belonged to someone in the Burmese immigrant village all-but opposite the bar. Lucy was the first to die.

'Excusez-moi.'
'Yup!' came from three self-assured wasted idiots (us).
'Your cat, she with snake,' the French couple tentatively relayed.

So this wasn't big news, Lucy batted the little worms around; Tiny Cat was surprisingly smart as kittens went and she kept a wide berth and the other cat was huge and hard enough to be half tiger. So what - but we went to see what was up.

Lucy was on a bamboo chair that had been left to rot outside the bar. In the shape of a 'd' the snake hung a metre over the wall behind, with an thigh-thick coil around Lucy's mid-section, the second turn of its articulated wrap of muscle was almost touching itself, closed far too tight around her neck. Of course it was far too late but the twitching foot, barely protruding from the bands of scales, brought out the 'protect the innocent' instinct out in us.

We passed the panicking girl a torch instructing, 'whatever you do keep us in the light'. Two steps back I picked up the only two implements, our 'bad customer machete' and a crowbar from the scrap metal heap. I chose the machete, my co-worker chose the crowbar.

The plan:

The girl would hold a strong beam of light on the snake's head, unshakingly and focused she was our beacon in the dangerous dark.

The guy to my right would pin the snake, which was currently shaping up to dislocate its own jaw over Lucy's head. The crowbar claw would be strong enough to hold the section that would be described as 'neck' into the bamboo chair backrest.

The final blow would be mine, I wasn't a fan of suffering in any way but I had a good idea what a snake this big did in a village this small - so I would make my choice. One slam behind the head and then, as my family had always told me, 'don't kill it if you're not planning on eating it'.

The reality:

It wasn't worth imagining the final stages of the machete blow, and although I brought that blade down hard and fast, things just didn't work out.

She held that light straight the true.

He slammed the crowbar hard into the side of the maybe-two-metre coil of muscle with teeth at one end and a life-ending supply of strength - so far so good, and as planned. . .

Then the ground around our feet moved on its own, contorting and arching as the extra two metres of python we hadn't accounted for rose up around our ankles.

A plan was still a plan and as the ground writhed around me I swung the machete down as hard as I could right where I thought would be most effective.

This was the moment the girl with the torch hit the floor. She had fallen a second before - actually fallen over in shock at the extra snake that was suddenly everywhere – but in this second, things went dark and in the two last flashes of light as the torch bounced out of her hand I saw the blade hit the snake right on the skull-cap.

The half-light of the torch rolling away lasted long enough for me to reel back to draw level with my accomplice, but he was metres away and getting further. It took one second more to find out where the snake's head was now, mostly because it wasn't in the same place as before. Now standing tall, face to face with me it was super pissed off, because I had hit it in the head with a big knife!

Things you learn living in the thick of it; snakes have a hard cap over their head that's way too thick to get through with a single blow.

They can also move fast and this one flew at me, it was kind-of incredible seeing it glide so fast with at least half of its body standing tall and its head close to face height with mine. I ran like a frog in a beehive, ducking under and rolling over anything to get as far away from the bitey end as I could.

It only turned back when I jumped the wall across the road, and then it just looped around in the middle of the road plunging back below the bar one more time. I was just relieved that it didn't decide to snap the horizontal girl's neck on its way.

A few days passed without doing much but telling people how crazy that moment was, and we kind-of forgot our vendetta against the snake right up until Tiny Cat disappeared.

The direct proportion of anger, to how small an animal is in relation to how big its killer was, works on almost anything apart from insects and fish; so the python eating Tiny Cat made everyone pretty livid.

I don't particularly get upset when bad things happen, I just plan really far ahead, so using the things we had lying around the bar I started on my 'bitey end containment device'. It was pretty basic: a long piece of wire folded in two and pushed down the middle of a length of inch-thick water pipe, the loose ends were then wrapped around a stick. The idea would be that the looped end would somehow go around the snake's neck and when someone pulled on the stick end, this loop would tighten. This piece of wire and pipe had lain in the corner of the bar for a week already - some internet searching told me that the snake was busy digesting 'something' and it could be another week or even longer until it showed itself again. The same searches made me a little more concerned about trying to catch this thing, bringing up articles where smaller pythons has killed and eaten fully grown men.

Don't get me wrong, I love animals – but if it was a trade-off between a snake and half the cats, some of the dogs and maybe a child or two, the snake was on the light side of the caring scale.

Chapter 49 – finally

It could have been my tenth trip out to the lagoon, sitting with a group who I knew quite well from the last week waiting out the rain at the bar. When we finally managed to get a warm day we took the opportunity. I had just told them that the waves were far too big to attempt the cliff jumping but if we tucked away inside the harbour on the other island we might catch the sunset without being knocked out of the boat.

We had been in the lagoon for a few hours and the world outside had turned itself up a few octaves, waves were now thumping up against the opening of the lagoon, a dull echo off the towering cliffs told Sid and me that the ride back was going to be rough, but not impossible.

We had to keep the party going; it was what we had been paid for so, with the music at full volume to power back in style, Sid angled his long tail to connect with the waves in the least confrontational way.

Ten metres into the open ocean the boat pulled back, twisting sideways into a wave and rolling violently. When we didn't pull forwards again to face the oncoming swell I knew something was wrong – climbing out of the covered front of the boat where everybody was bracing themselves against the sides I saw Sid wrestling with the counter-balanced handle of the boat, the propeller on the other end, sticking two meters from the bow of the boat. It had tangled into huge lengths thick black bundles of fishing net and became even more so with every wave.

'Kim!' he hollered over the noise of the wind and the revving engine, 'Hold him!' handing the handle of the levered motor to me, so I could push down and keep the propeller end out of the water. The little man crouched – knife in mouth, getting his hands as far along the shaft as he could reach and made an attempt at climbing down the length without touching the water. The back of the boat slammed the surface with a clap and Sid fell in the sea.

'Sid!' I lurched forward just as he came up, letting the shaft come down right by his head. He grabbed on to it again, moving slowly to the far end, the ocean smashing him into the pole and lifting the boat with each wave. Sid started sawing away at the net with his knife.

They were illegal fishing nets, put over the mouth of the lagoon to catch sea life on its way out with the falling tide, so I didn't feel bad about cutting them open. The next wave dropped from its peak and with it, the entire back of the boat dropped also, pushing Sid deep under the black surface of the swell. He came back up with net across his face, struggling to get through it and grab a fresh breath, hacking away at the strings. By the time we had dragged him back onto the boat he was a choking wreck, but still half laughing

'Kim, I think we have problem Kim'.

The next plan was to drop the shaft vertically into the sea, so it wasn't slapping the surface with the rolling waves. I checked on my guests telling them about the engine problems, but not really in detail, they seemed fine - with enough drinks and music, most people are.

We took turns to climb hand-over-hand down the shaft under the water to try and cut a bit more net off each time, feeling the water rush up and down as the surge pushed us deeper and then turned to heave us roughly skywards, numb fingers struggling to grip both the metal pole and the knife – until finally the boat broke free, drifting and rolling once more into the waves.

So this is why I was still remotely sober at 8am, sitting alone in the bar, video chatting with a friend. A noise that was hard to mistake, 'whhhtchhh-meo!' came up through the floorboards below my feet.

'I've got to go, I think the snake just grabbed a cat under the bar.'

On my belly with my head under the bathroom steps I squinted into the darkness, something was moving but it wasn't close enough to make out. Then that familiar ring of scaled muscle caught a slice of light between the boards, revolving around its prey – the third cat was hard to make out now as most of its body had already been enveloped.

I grabbed my snake catcher and started to poke it in under the steps, the snake raised its head into the void between us, turning to stone and fixing its stare on the intruding object. I would need help, or at least someone to pry this thing off my throat if things went wrong – so I took the risk and, laying the bitey end containment device down in an attempt to keep the snake's attention, I ran to drag my friend out of bed.

So once again I pushed the bent wire through the pipe, making the ring on the other end as large as possible. As planned the snake pushed its head out into the space between the blue pipe and its prey, squaring off in preparation to lash out - I dropped the pipe down in front of its face and the wire loop followed it right over the snake's neck.

Pull! I yanked the metal wire against the pipe and the backlash was immense - jerking the pipe almost right out of my hands. I panicked and with all my body weight rocked back and tried to pull the snake out from under the bar, through the gap in the steps and into the bathroom.

It seems that snakes poising for attack don't grip onto things as hard as when they already have prey in their coils, so the whole thing followed much easier than imagined, bringing its head right out of the gap and into the light. Chaos ensued as the python, like four metres of slippery bicep, hit the walls, the urinals, the pipes and fought to get a wrap around any part of us it could.

Grateful that I had the bitey-end on the end of a stick, I pushed it down against the floor as hard as possible - over the slaps and hisses I could hear the plastic popping and fracturing under the sideways pressure. While I was pinning it in place my friend grabbed a bar knife and somehow I managed to keep the snakes head down long enough for him to get under the throat – it didn't take long to take its head from its body.

Chapter 50 – snakebeque

She woke up. Fresher than the rest of us on any given day she had managed to sleep past midday, but it was still early enough to be sure that everyone on the night shift of this 'open 24/7' bar would be passed out in a puddle of something somewhere. She would drink something with caffeine, and then something with gin – it would be enough to stay awake until someone else surfaced.

This was when she saw the fridge full of blood.

I knew already knew, from my snake-catching research, that a Burmese Python, especially a four metre long one, can continue to fight, bite and wrap around prey for quite some time after it has been decapitated – the nerve endings of such a prehistoric creature were still firing off in the bag we'd put it in - even though it's head was sitting on the bar top meters away.

The snake had managed to burst its severed stub out of the plastic bag somehow, and in the tail-end of its nervous system's reaction to attack, it had straightened out and spun, smashing its way around the bottom three shelves of the glass fronted fridge, and consequently covering everything in blood.

With 'maybe they killed someone' in her mind, she performed a unique feat of her own Island Eyes, turning her back on a fridge that was dripping with blood and starting her day as per usual – making a strong drink - anything that wasn't pre-chilled really.

'Mr Kim where go, mai?' she massage girls sang from the shade.

'I've got a big snake to cook,' I felt honesty was the best policy when you had almost four metres of dead snake filling almost an entire black trash bag.

'Have what?'

'The big snake.'

'Snake?'

It was easier this way, I reached into the bag and pulled a loop out, my hand barely showing on both sides of its girth. The girls scattered as if it was alive and launching itself their way.

The restaurant that would normally cook a fish if you brought it to them took one look and held up their hands, 'No!' they were laughing in disbelief but also adamant, 'Not cook here, him big snake.'

If you kill it you should eat it – options became limited around the island. I went back to the bar to do it myself.

Six pm in the red light bouncing across the ocean, two boys wiped bloody streaks into their sweat as they brushed away the flies. The flies that had been attracted by the four metre python getting butchered on the floor.

A quick cut down from a severed neck, maybe six inches, and with one gripping the exposed section, the other twisting both sets of fingers into the loose collar of skin, and each leaning his whole body weight back, they pulled away from each other.

A tear, like popping bubble wrap underwater, showing minimal blood, the skin folded back onto itself gripping harder as we passed the midsection and easing off towards the tail - scaly skin left flesh and a light pink snake was born from its dark scarred exterior. The bones jutted in natural rigor mortis twists and contorted muscles wrapped up its entire length.

The skin was magnificent, un-tearable and impossible to fold flat. We flung one end over the rafter across the centre of the bar and wiped up the fallout after it dropped its half-length down the other side.

The flesh would be cooked somehow! We sawed it off the spiked bone with the same serrated kitchen knife that slit its throat and piled it onto plates in fillet shape chunks - I followed online instructions as we kneaded salt and pepper into the sinews and beat the pieces with a peg hammer.

Sparks flew as each piece hit the grid just inches from the simmering coals. Snake doesn't brown it just darkens as it cooks, piling up to one side of the bbq – we offered anyone who passed-by a taste of the exotic.

'I tried to make something unique,' I explained, 'using the apes as a building block.'

'Oh, I can see that, because of the hands right?'

'Yep, pretty much, but their brains are wired for creativity,' I thought about the best way to explain this, 'so the animals ... I didn't make them exactly how they are now,' I tried, 'maybe I made twenty types of horse, and some didn't survive. Sometimes it was just a bad design, and sometimes just because they had to share a space with something that ate them all.'

'A bad design?' she asked.

'Sure, like the stripy horse here,' I pointed to a vast space on the east side of Africa, 'I put him all over the place, but now you can only find them where the long grass is, because they hide amongst it using their stripes.'

'But there are hundreds of different types of horse creatures, you said you made twenty and some didn't survive, so ...?'

'Yes, so that's the thing, if two different types of horses met and reproduced they can make a third type, which is kind-of a mix of the two types,' I was briefly explaining something very complex, 'and maybe this horse, because it's a mix of two that could survive in this area of the globe, maybe it's an even stronger horse than both of its parents.'

'So you didn't make all the animals, sometimes they make themselves?'

'Yes, often, so the ones we can see now are quite different from the ones I put there.'

'And the humans?' she pulled me back onto her line of questioning.

'I put many types of humans, some were much more advanced than others. The ones which were more like the apes, they didn't survive at all. I don't know why, maybe they lost something that the apes needed to survive, but didn't quite have what it took to be human.'

'That's so brutal! So the first real humans to survive were the ones we can see now?'

'Not so much, some of the other's survived for a long time, and I think some of them cross-bred, but these ones are the ones that are here at the moment. It's because they build so much,' I laughed, 'but you should see the stories they come up with when they find some of my early work!'

Chapter 51 – pick up and go

The closer the year crept towards its end, the more vivid the setting sun caught the cloud banks that, in winter, seemed to lay low to the west between the islands – giving us the perfect place to bob and watch.

I had been running trips once or twice a week without the risk of high winds or rain sweeping in, the nagging feeling that even these windows were coming to an end had been showing itself through the past week, this being the only day in a fortnight that I had managed to take a group out.

These days in the ocean and every night in the bar were mounting up and pressing on my exhaustion levels, It was the stress free approach to things that was keeping it all going – not worrying about working too hard, nor working too little – just doing what I had to do, essentially just staying alive for the low season.

Eat once, drink twice, breathe ... and protect my delusions at all costs. Above all it was immensely liberating and easier than you would think, if you never plan ahead. I preferred it this way. Keep your future gaze at a two hour limit and you will see that you have nothing to worry about.

Darkness came and we tied the boat up on the shore and bid the guests farewell for now. The silence was perfect; my long but calming stroll down the beach towards the jungle walk had become a satisfying ritual of self-reflection between an active day and intoxicating night. I laughed at myself, and all the

times I've wasted doing things that I didn't want to. Did I even know how many hours I have to live? Not many of us do, each minute was part of everything you will ever know. As my mind wandered, so did I, and finally up the hill to the bar. 'Hello?'
Empty.

Not a soul in sight.

The huts, gutted out. The stock abandoned. No signs of a forced removal, just a total 'pick up and go'.

Chapter 52 – dangerous accusations

'They were selling Yaba'

'The High Bar?'

'Yes, they all left the island yesterday,' the bartender obviously didn't know I had been helping out there for months, 'their big boss would definitely have something to say,' he smiled a little, but not much, everybody knew the consequences of this crime.

'They fled the island on a wooden boat, nobody knows where they went.'

A lot of people were talking about it, how the High Bar had either upset their big boss, or they were caught for selling meth, or this, or that.

The rumours about Yaba weren't true, of course, but stories can get you killed out here.

Nobody seemed to be focusing on me, maybe because I was always around and not often behind the bar, but a few people were certain they had heard from someone who had heard from someone that the whole team were hiding out in Laos.

I didn't care, What peace of mind I had was once again derailed and my only way of survival took yet another knock, a sick discontent as my gut warning me about things to come crept in.

Lemon – scene 19

'So they think that they're created,' Lemon put one open hand out to her side, 'or they think they evolved,' she put the other out to match it.

'Yes, pretty much.'

'Which one?'

'Both, it's funny, most of them believe that they evolved and the others all believe that they were made like they are, but not many of them know that I made them and then they just adapted.'

'That is funny,' Lemon burst out a laugh that tipped the waves white and moved the treetops along one side of the island, 'the people are so ridiculous.'

I didn't know how to agree with her more, they were, but maybe we had different opinions of why, but it didn't matter. The people were ridiculous in their need to think that they were more than just ... things.

The crab – episode 5

From the heavens, with no warning or build-up, a hard hot wind dug deep into the ocean ahead. So much so that the flip flop stood at an angle with just the crab's weight on the tip stopping it from flipping over, end over end. He clamped into the foam rubber holding as tight as he could as the entire course of his vessel was forced into a change of direction.

The wake that had been trailing its 'V' shape from the heel end of the shoe reversed itself and, with not only the crab and the straps acting as a sail, but the ocean itself surging with it, the journey was heading in this newfound direction at triple speed.

Salt spray still overlapped from behind and the surface had lost its glassy transparency. At a time like this a crab can only think 'oh well' and hold tight. In the unpredictability of the middle of ocean he could only be glad to be travelling somewhere, anywhere at all.

Chapter 53 – run

It came in the night, the final feeling. It's over.
I just stood there in the dark room sweating and aching and impassively letting my brain play out options – the walls seemed thick and heavy around me. With the accusations, the brewing feeling that some sort of end was adamant, whether it be above or below ground, the world outside the walls didn't hang any lighter.

I borrowed some money from a close friend, stuffed it deep into the rice bag pushing everything down on top of it. I never had a watch or a phone to keep track of the passing minutes so I took the liberty of 'taking the time' and permanently borrowed a cheap plastic tick-tock alarm clock off a shelf outside a shop on pier road - if I could keep the battery from falling out it would work.

The first boat off the island moved slowly, I didn't speak to anyone the entire way to the mainland. I didn't even look back at the island disappearing behind me.

Two feet on the shore, I walked past the first clamouring salespeople pushing Bangkok, Pattaya and Changmai. A motorbike to the bus terminal it was, rice bag sandwiched between my chest and his back, toes clipping the tar – piano played in my mind.
I studied a map of the Thai border running my eyes around the perimeter, red and black dashes indicating checkpoints and immigration control stops. Nine in a row en-route to Cambodia. Closed borders to Burma.

What's this? A border town, Satun, with the checkpoint 'Wang Prachan' crossing into Malaysia. It looked remote.

I asked the squat salesman for 'the local bus to Satun kap' and paid a pittance for the ticket. Stopping at every village, and keeping me off the radar, the bus wandered its way to the city - all eyes on me as the only non-Thai riding south this way.

I made it to Satun, starving and in complete darkness. Knowing I should find a place to sleep I started that familiar street walk down the main streets. I knew deep down this wouldn't be so easy as reception lights were either off or switching off, but I had a fold of notes in the back of my bag that could be the bribe, or ticket over this border, or a target on my back. Sleeping on remote Thai city streets is a really good way to get robbed in the night, so I figured spending something on a room was necessary.

There was one other person checking in at the last minute cheap hotel - I found it by following a light up a side street - it must have been close to my last chance. The girl also seemed flustered, dropping things and struggling to find her passport in the bottom of her rucksack.

'Passport?' this might be a small problem, I hung back and watched as she handed it over; the reception staff leafed through it, past her photo page giving a quick glance up and then to her visas - this was definitely bad news. Since when was a valid visa needed to stay at a hotel? Maybe for remote border towns where they had a lot of problems or maybe they would pick up a commission for turning people over to the police – it wasn't worth the risk.

I had to try. 'Just your cheapest room please'

'400 baht, kaa,' I went for my money but she continued, 'passport, kaa.'

'I don't have one, it was stolen,' I tried.

'Not have passport, not have room for you.'

The reception assistant appeared and the main desk lady handed him the girl's key.

I hesitated, my mind throwing options around inside itself – the girl to my right leant close to me showing me her mobile phone screen, saying, 'Maybe this is a good place to stay.'

She was smart and she was lying, right in front of the staff. Her phone was open on the notes page where she had typed 'You can share with me. Meet me outside :)'

'Okay that looks great,' I answered, keeping up the charade, 'thanks.'

She followed the reception assistant up the stairs and I did as I was told and waited for her in the street - you find the good in people in the most unlikely places.

Chapter 54 – no-man's land

I look down at my feet, soft grey with street dust, dark patches showing through from two years of holes and scars - flip-flops holding themselves together with twisted and knotted straws threaded into the split soles and rubber fittings. My rice bag, almost empty, stood up on its low centre of gravity - I had scrunched the open top together and twisted some rubber cord around it for added security, the irony being that the state of me and my luggage made me almost unapproachable, let alone a lucrative target.

Then it was there, at the crest of a rise in the road, the Thai border appeared just twenty metres ahead of me. Two gates guarded by two men on each, one for coming into Thailand and the other for entering into a stretch of no-mans-land before you were stamped into Malaysia.

The queue to leave Thai soil stayed at around ten people, with new people joining it as others showed their passports and walked through. The guards were armed but stood at ease, their eyes scanning the scene on both sides of the borderline. I still wasn't sure what I would be doing, but I was becoming increasingly aware that if my luck failed now, it would be a long time before I left this country.

The air was close and the sun relentless. I picked up my sack and took a few steps forward before setting it down again. I repeated this three times or more before my nerves told me to stop, breathe and collect myself. I knew what would happen if I showed my passport anywhere near here, and although I hadn't discounted the idea of trying the 'plead ignorance' route I had already stuffed my passport deep into my bag mentally accepting that I was going to try something stupid instead.

My break was a stress-wank. Five minutes in the public toilets to the right of the queue, pushed the nerves down a little but I knew myself and this clarity window would close within the next ten minutes. Still it gave me room to breathe and reassess.

Back at the gates I stood in the same spot, people filed past in disorder right up to the checkpoint where the disorganisation suddenly became unsettlingly strict for someone who needed to find another way through. Trying to pass the line would be extremely unlikely and if seen I would be stopped, checked and arrested for illegal entry. Not a good outcome, worse when they find my passport with my two years expired visa.

I had to do something. This is the border crossing - two fences, maybe two hundred metres of 'no-man's-land' apart from each other and each fence stretching away into the distance from either side of their control points; letting people in, letting people out.

I stood facing the 'no man's land' – incredibly there was a market in there – a market held by locals to take advantage of the tourist's obsession with duty-free goods, a great place to sell something at the normal price and let westerners think they were getting a good deal maybe.

I realised I had been standing still watching for too long - soon it would be a red flag if someone noticed my nerves - which had since returned. Off to my left, on the Thai side of the border, was a fruit market, so I walked around amongst the fruit sellers, trying to get a better idea of the layout of the Duty-Free market just through the fence – the salespeople had to get themselves and their stock to the market between the borders somehow.

Just then, with the fence to my right and my back to the checkpoint, I noticed a folded stall on wheels rolling behind the fruit stands heading towards the border. I was just wondering how they would get through the security checkpoint with such a big cart when, true to my thoughts, right in-front of my eyes, about four metres of the security fence started shifting. Two men from the market had unhooked a section of the chain link and lifted it to move it aside, the rolling table of baked goods pushed forward without slowing, heading for the gap.

It was better not to think; I made a bee-line towards the cart, passing behind it as it moved forwards. It was still about five metres from the opening and I was maybe ten paces behind, I aligned the cart between myself and the two men, who were paying little attention, and I tried to look busy fiddling with my clothing and intermittently checking my pockets, just in case someone else was watching. I didn't know what I was going to do once through, but keeping my mind blank and trying to keep my cool I passed the open end of the fence to my left just as the cart rolled through on my right – it blocked me from the view of the two men who were already back on both ends of the removed section ready to lift it back into place.

The border security had been mostly hidden by the fruit market on the Thai side of the fence, but now I could see them again, one officer facing each way, they scanned the bustle in front of them.

Still walking, with apparent confidence, I ducked a little, but not so much as to look suspicious, and kept in place - eclipsing myself behind the cart from their watchful eyes. The further away I got; the faster I walked – when the stall abruptly stopped I just kept going, now it wasn't worth looking back, I was too far in for excuses.

With sweat dripping into my eyes I found a shady space to recollect my nerves, already through one checkpoint, but a long walk from the other, I knew that I couldn't *legally* go either way. The road through the mid-border section seemed far too long, swimming in the rising heat – I couldn't take too much time, I was already struggling to breathe right, and the mounting pressure was pushing nerves into uncertainty; not something I could afford to feel right then.

The dusty road to the Malay check-in wasn't so far but every step felt like the second hand ticking – taking a little too long each time.

The entry to 'no-man's-land' from Malaysia was on the left and the entry into Malaysia was to the right. The guards stood on each side of the exit, both facing the queue filing to stamp their way into their country. This side of the fence the gap was wider, busy and noticeably less intense than the Thai entry to 'no-man's-land' - this made sense, seeing as people filing through from this direction has already been through the main security check on their way out of Thailand, and they were only needing an entry stamp.

I just kept walking towards them, knowing this wasn't the case for me, but still having to get to the other side one way or another. With waterfalls sliding down my sides and my heart pressing on my jugular I finally reached the semi-organised cluster, hanging back to let a small group go in front of me, I lost my nerve right in front of the first security guard, turning an unplanned right. It wasn't a good idea, scolding myself 'is there another way to look more suspicious? Maybe I should try that as well!'

Further back now, I followed the fence between the 'in' and the 'out' openings with my eyes. The only way through was a gap behind the 'in' booth, and that meant passing the guard I'd just bailed in front of and there was no doubt that someone walking behind the booth would warrant being stopped.

I had made a mistake, getting this far and potentially being caught would send me into a world of legal trouble and I would no doubt find myself inside a cell for some time. I had to get to the other side of that fence before I let my brain take over and I lost my nerve completely - I cut through into the line of people coming into no-man's-land from Malaysia, still busy fussing with their passports as they left the entry point and readying themselves to cross to the Thai side. Right here I took my chance and turned against the tide, waving to a friend who didn't exist and, with the air of someone who might have forgotten something and was just running back for it - I walked the wrong way through the danger zone and out the other side of the 'in' checkpoint.

Passing the guard I patted my pockets and faux looked around - he was facing towards Malaysia, of course, expecting anyone who was crossing the border illegally to be coming from that direction – after all, who would smuggle themselves into Malaysia once they had already been officially checked coming out through the Thai exit checkpoint. Unless they were me.

Faking a slight rush and checking my pockets once more, I made out that I may have even forgotten or lost something further back, and removed myself from the guards' line of sight as quickly as possible by crossing behind the same style toilet block that stood on the other side.

I was in Malaysia - but still not convinced I was free and clear, because I hadn't dared to look back I wasn't sure my actions hadn't been noticed, so I kept my head down and powered down the long downhill slope winding away from the scene of the crime.

Chapter 55 – the side roads

'I am looking for a bus terminal to go to Kuala Lumpur,' earned me the same directions back to the checkpoint where the pre-booked busses stood waiting for anyone who had legitimately made it through immigration – not an intelligent place to return to even if I could just pay the driver to take me to K.L.

I tacked, 'but not that one' onto the end of my request, but with no luck, it seemed that this was my only obvious options.

'Fifty ringgit Alor Setar.' The boy I had asked last couldn't have been older than twelve.

'Fifty ringgit to Alor Setar?' I repeated, pretending I knew what an Alor Setar was.

'Yes sir, Alor Setar take fly to Kuala Lumpur,' he motioned across the road to a small layby, of course it would be a scrambler motorbike.

I didn't like the idea of flying before I needed to, but if there were flight connections then there would be bus options. I had no idea how far Alor Setar was but I knew I had to keep moving. 'I only have Thailand money,' I told him.

'500 Thai baht,' he told me, I knew this was more than 50 Malaysian Ringgit but I accepted anyway and climbed onto the back of the bike.

It was maybe a kilometre down the road where we came across two army personnel pulling bikes and cars over for what was presumably a contraband search, as we came close the car they had just checked pulled away and one of the soldiers waved our bike into the side of the road, of course the kid stopped. The men seemingly had no problem with the obvious age of the driver but asked us to dismount anyway. I did as I was told, my legs feeling like jelly as I stepped onto the hot ground, they asked to present my passport.

I knew it was over.

Digging deep in the rice bag I handed my passport over, trying to control my expression as one of the men leafed through my pages obviously checking my legality. The moment he realised I was illegally here I would be in serious trouble. He was going back and forth, looking each page up and down and, presumably, thinking he had missed my visa on the first glance. He asked, 'You stay in Malaysia long time?'

I dug for an answer and tried, 'No, I leave today.' 'When did you come into Malaysia?'

I tried the truth, 'Today, just now,' I pointed back up the road.

He looked puzzled, turning pages again, obviously not expecting me to have smuggled myself across the border and just performing the normal checks when they pull someone over.

The other soldier pointed to my bag, spoke Malaysian to his colleague and then asked, 'It's your bag?'

'Yes,' I replied, 'my bag broke so I am using a rice sack,' trying to laugh it off. The first man must have realised the visa was indeed missing because he also started speaking Malaysian and flipping through my passport pages dramatically, showing the second man each page – the second man nodded a lot and placed one hand on my bag as if he were about the search it.

Both things were bad news. Firstly they would find all my money in cash stuffed into a rice sack - the border control police weren't known for their honesty. Secondly they had a very good reason to put handcuffs on me now, the money and my freedom would be gone before we made it to a police station.

A car roared around the corner behind me, tearing a column of dust up behind it as it screeched into view and chased the noise of its own acceleration down the road hurtling past at a breakneck speed. The air was brown with flying grit and the hot wind hit the four of us in its wake, I looked to the soldiers for their reaction. They were already half-way to their jeep, my passport lying on top of my rice bag, my possessions untouched.

'We can take the side roads?' I suggested.

This didn't seem like a problem. 'We go through the villages,' the boy said, starting the bike again and waiting for me to un-stick my feet from the ground and hop back on. He turned a sharp left down a mid-size track thirty metres along the road and another hard right onto a smaller path, stretching straight through the trees, glowing red-gold in line in the afternoon sun.

The bike threatened to shake itself apart, speeding down the degraded Malaysian side-roads. Skidding on corners and almost completely losing control on loose stones we skipped from bank to bank over the dugout wheel ruts trying to avoid potholes. With the light flashing between the trees and the taste of dust on my tongue, we seemed to fly for hours.

The sun made tracks through the sky as the hours slid by, my possessions bouncing in the bag at every unpredictable speed-bump. I knew my skin was burning but I couldn't feel it for the passing air – glowing smog in the distance sat thick, promising a city on the horizon - if we didn't obliterate ourselves in oncoming traffic before we made it that far.

Welcome to Alor Setar, the city of nothing much. My young driver dropped me close to the centre, looking much like any developed south-east Asian city. I paid him and then realised I had no real idea why I was here. It had been a good idea to get away from the checkpoint-ridden border roads and to somewhere with bus stations and cheap motels, but as of this moment I had no idea if Alor Setar was any better for me than, well, any other place.

I knew that if I was going to get out of this country I had to go via Kuala Lumpur. Of course I would need to fly eventually, but with no visa stamp it would be a very unlikely and dangerous attempt.

I checked for the time - the battery had fallen loose from that useless tick-tock clock and it was no use resetting it now as it would just shake loose again. I walked around the main roads of the city, catching any shade I could so as not to layer more sunburn on what I already had, until finally I found some sort of terminal.

The sign, written in green marker pen and tacked to the inside of a glass booth, read: 'Kuala Lumpur Sleeper 35RM' which I guess is around 7 euros or 8 dollars. It didn't say how you would be getting there or the times it left, or how long it took.

I booked it: 'Leaving?' 'Tomorrow morning at 4am.' 'Arriving?' '2pm.' Ten hours, okay, I can walk the night away and sleep on the ... oh wait, I didn't ask what I would be travelling on.

4am rolled around and with tired feet I re-found the terminal, boarded a minivan and, assuming the sleeping would be done sitting upright, I settled in for a long trip. Ten minutes later the minivan stopped at a small train station where we were herded off and into a train carriage lined with bunk beds.

Small yoga mat style shelves actually, but an amazing lie-down none-the-less - right up until my bunkmate joined me. Ah yes, two people per single bed, and this guy was a sticky one. Very sweaty!
But I guess I couldn't complain too much.

Chapter 56 - breathe

I was in mindless autopilot, where stress should be at a high but I had been gritting my teeth for too long and acceptance took over. There was no doubt that a tenfold of anxiety was on its way so my mind had boiled the journey down to 'just something that had to happen first'.

I was in no danger right now, walking the streets of Kuala Lumpur following the signs, to the over-ground-underground train station, that hung above the city. Days travel from the checkpoints and foot by foot making my way towards the final stop, the international airport. At this point, I had no idea what I would be doing when I got there but I didn't need to sweat over that right now.

The culture was cleaner compared to Thailand, I knew because of the way they eyed the dirtbag with burns, bruises and a ricebag under his arm, sweating his way around their capital.

I must have been tired because every blink lasted seconds and gave me a little relief. Bottled anxiety could also explain this retreat from reality. I would have to eat; it had been a day and a half.

Malaysia has these amazing bags of sloppy meat that they sell on the side of any cheap side-street. White dough closed around some 'maybe-pork' sat under a lukewarm lamp, each around the size of two clasped hands. My immune system, by now, was near indestructible.

'Two of these please.'

'Char siew Pao?'

'Okay...'
'One ringgit twenty.'
'... okay.'

My greasy fingers pushed the spare change into the Metro system and the over-ground train shook me all the way to the central station from where I took an express train in the direction of the airport, where I would most likely be detained for travelling without visa documentation. I arrived too fast, the comfort of the autopilot ended and a small feed of uncomfortable adrenaline set in.

Now what?

I walked around. It was considerably cooler inside the terminal, people went about their business, the huge screens changed intermittently and the intercom reminded us to stay with our baggage. What now?

Of course I was going to try and fly - I wouldn't have wandered here if I wasn't, but the thought was still sickening. Most of me assumed that of course without a visa someone simply cannot leave, but still willing to try, I bought a drink at an airport café so I could use the standalone computer.

The internet gave me my two options; deportation; being returned to the country you came from, or a court date to argue your case as an illegal immigrant. My nationality was on my side here, with a British passport and no Thai visas in the previous years the Malaysian authorities would be unlikely to send me to Bangkok, but I would still have to explain how I had got here. The court date came with fines, probable holding-cell prison time, possibly caning which is still a normal legal form of minor punishment in Malaysia, and the process could take months or more.

Two days until Christmas wasn't the best time to let my family know I was trying to illegally cross a second border in a week. If I didn't contact them again they would fear the worst, and the worriers amongst them would have a terrible time.

I contacted one of my brothers.

It started with, 'I need a favour, I'm in Malaysia, don't ask how but I don't have a visa ...' and ended with him saying, 'Okay, I'll buy you a morning flight to London, try and get on it somehow.'

Chapter 57 – cold sweat

The middle aged couple side glanced at me. From their perspective this must have been bizarre. I had been in the bathroom washing myself so that at least the grime was a little dispersed - standing in the hand-wash station wiping myself down with wet toilet paper gathered good reactions, but not as much as tampering with your passport in the airport.

That was the plan - to fly out of here early in the morning, claiming that I was in fact inside my allocated visa time but that the stamp had been damaged by damp. I found the stamp from my visa runs to Malaysia on the 21st of December, two years before, and now all I had to do it make it look like it was possibly a recent addition.

My spit softened the page and my fingernail picked away at the dates - I made the spine of the passport wet with saliva leaving a wet patch where the year and part of the month were printed on that specific entry stamp, then closed the passport and sat on it for around twenty minutes. The couple had transitioned from glances to staring.

When the spit had dried the pages together I pulled them open quickly in the hope that it would look like the same natural damp damage that had made the edge of the entry stamp unreadable. The first few attempts worked quite well, and finally after an hour of picking and spitting I couldn't make out the numbers. It was a plan so ridiculous that it might even work.

Then came a sleepless night, my pillow was a bundled up cloth I had used to dry myself with a few days before, but minutes after laying my head on it the mould spores had half closed my throat.

The tiny tick-tock alarm clock still hadn't earned my trust and even though I set it for 7am and lay beside it on the floor, every time I woke up I walked to check the time on the big screens, this might have happened every twenty minutes.

Finally it wasn't worth sleeping; I met a zombie in the mirror. Black sunken eyes, stains on the skin that wouldn't wash off and clothes that by now just hung overstretched and filthy.

It was time.

The queue shortened to nothing, my excuses rolled around my mind. 'Similan islands' 'working on boats' - I wasn't sure which direction I would go.

I had chosen carefully, with five lines to join and knowing Malaysia's reputation for sexism I chose the line with the biggest, fattest, most decorated man squatting behind the customs desks. I was hoping for some bending of the rules here and I knew that it was less likely for a woman to risk it, because if something went wrong her punishment would be much more severe than that of a man, and this man looked like he had some rule-bending power.

There I stood, rice bag by my side, ticket in hand and a passport crumpled and corrugated from the water damage, sliding across the desk. The officer took his time. He squinted, shook his head and left the desk taking my passport with him. A few drops of sweat left my fingertips.

He came back, shaking his head again. 'I can't find your passport stamp.'

'It's there,' I told him, 'I just arrived.'

'From where did you arrive?' he asked.

'The Similan islands, I've been working on a boat, but I've got to go home for family reasons.'

'On a boat?'

'Yes, hence the passport,' I indicated to the state it was in.

'Where did you enter the country?' His instant replies set me more on edge.

'At the docks, on the west coast,' I tried to keep my story close to the truth so I could remember it if I had to repeat it to someone else. I kept a straight face, everything below the counter prickled cold with sweat.

'You gave them your passport?'

'Yes, at the marina.'

'Ah!' he put his forehead in his hand, 'Then there is the problem.'

'The problem?' I asked, feigning surprise, confused at a moment of absolute sexual arousal!

'Yes, it can happen, the immigration at the small port did not stamp you to arrive.'

'I think the stamp is there, maybe it's just hard to read.'

'This one?' he pointed at my doctored stamp, 'this one is from before, it has an exit stamp.'

Oh hell, the exit stamp, I hadn't even thought about it, and I assume the officer hadn't noticed the date discrepancy. 'Yes, from before I went to the Similan islands,' I lied. 'So they didn't give me a new stamp?'

'No, there is no stamp,' he looked deadpan, then sighed, 'I can see you were here not so long ago.'

'Yes, just a few weeks,' I tried, knowing this would make me legal if he didn't investigate further.

'And you will leave Malaysia now?'

'Yes.'

'It's better you do not return, I will stamp your passport to say you have to leave.'

'I won't be coming back,' I assured, 'that would be amazing, thank you.'

'It's not normal' he said, looking me up and down. I knew a bribe was what was normal, but the state of me must have told him that I wasn't carrying a lot of money. 'So you can go now.'

A wave of relief, I thanked him again as I quickly snatched up my rice bag and passed the checkpoint, without looking back in case he had a change of heart I walked as far away as I could, hoping that out of sight would mean out of mind.

That was it; here I was, queuing to board a plane to England, a valid deportation in my hands and a boarding pass in the other.

The feeling when the plane lifted from the tarmac was a life bump in itself, or maybe just relief releasing adrenaline.

The plane passed over the palm oil plantations outside of Kuala Lumpur, turned in the sky, and roared sixteen hours across the world – homeward bound.

The crab – episode 6

The lack of whistling and flecks of salt spattering his shell was an exhilarating relief. A little heat was even penetrating through with the air creeping under his shell. The crab lifted himself up from his belly-squat against the flip-flop, he hadn't moved in days as the algae imprint indicated.

The scene slid into focus, from top to bottom. The bleached sky faded to crisp blue as his eyes adjusted to the sun. Palm trees stood stoic atop the layer upon layer of limestone slabs that circled a bay he knew well. A calm murmur carried in the breeze.

Mast tops swung gently, sails wrapped and protected from a recent change in the wind, but the ocean around them sparkled as it always did after it had been tormented.

Tiny fish caught his eye as he looked down into the shallows, that familiar shade of almost white that danced through the hatching left by the sun finishing its own journey, right there on the sea bed.

A rise and fall of a lapping tide let the crab breathe easily for the first time in a long time, a lump in his throat that he didn't know was there, dispersed and evaporated in the calm of the moment.

The flip-flop touched the sand with a soft bump, pulled away and returned, this time grounding and pivoting with each lap. The crab scuttled off. Home!

**Thank You for reading
Island Eyes
by CLEM**

**If you enjoyed this book please leave a review on
Amazon or Goodreads.
Reviews really help authors published by indie
publishers and helps other readers find good books
when they are looking for them**

Catch-Up with Clem at

@clem_worldwide

on Instagram or Twitter

See his Author page on Amazon and
Pendown Publishing.co.uk

This book is also available in eformats from

Amazon and PendownPubishing.co.uk

Lightning Source UK Ltd.
Milton Keynes UK
UKHW011957050220
358230UK00001B/20